Thinking Wi

Thinking Window Verses

By Kim Ryŏ

Translated by
Won-Chung Kim
Christopher Merrill
Lee Hyeonwu

Homa & Sekey Books
Paramus, New Jersey

FIRST EDITION

Copyright © 2024 by Homa & Sekey Books
English translation copyright © 2024 by Won-Chung Kim, Christopher Merrill, and Lee Hyeonwu
Cover art: Chae Jongki

All rights reserved. No part of this book may be reproduced, stored in a retrieval system, or transmitted in any form, or by any means, electronic, mechanical, photocopying, recording or otherwise, without prior permission from the publisher.

Library of Congress Cataloging-in-Publication Data

Names: Kim, Ryŏ, 1766-1822, author. | Kim, Won-Chung, 1959- translator. | Merrill, Christopher, translator. | Lee, Hyeonwu, 1958- translator.
Title: Thinking window verses / by Kim Ryŏ ; translated by Won-Chung Kim, Christopher Merrill, and Lee Hyeonwu.
Other titles: Sayuakpu. English

Identifiers: LCCN 2023043503 | ISBN 9781622461158 (paperback)
Subjects: LCGFT: Poetry.
Classification: LCC PL989.415.Y5 S3913 2024
 | DDC 895.71/2--dc23/eng/20240102
LC record available at https://lccn.loc.gov/2023043503

Published by Homa & Sekey Books
3rd Floor, North Tower
Mack-Cali Center III
140 E. Ridgewood Ave.
Paramus, NJ 07652

Tel: 201-261-8810, 800-870-HOMA
Fax: 201-261-8890
Email: info@homabooks.com
Website: www.homabooks.com

Printed in the USA
1 3 5 7 9 10 8 6 4 2

Acknowledgements

This work was supported by the English Translation of 100 Korean Classics program through the Ministry of Education of the Republic of Korea and the Korean Studies Promotion Service of the Academy of Korean Studies (AKS-2015-KCL-1230004).

Contents

Acknowledgements / v

Translators' Preface / ix

Introduction / xi

Thinking Window Verses **/ 001**

Preface / 003

Poems (1-300) / 005-339

Afterword / 340

About the Translators / 341

Translators' Preface

Tamjŏng Kim Ryŏ's *Thinking Window Verses* is a remarkable work of memory and imagination, a diaristic compendium of the people and places the poet encountered at the turn of the 19th century in Puryŏng, a town near the Chinese border in present-day North Korea, where he served the first of two five-year terms of exile. It was during his second term, in the southeastern port of Chinhae, present-day Changwon, South Korea, where part of the U.S. Commander Naval Fleet Korea is based, that he wrote three hundred poems, each of which begins with the question: "I ask, what do you think / of our beloved northern seaside?" The various answers he provides reveal a surprisingly modern sensibility, a clear-eyed vision of a world he came to love, notwithstanding his loneliness and despair. For Kim Ryŏ was an uncommonly empathetic figure, who took the measure of the people he met and transformed his experiences with them into poetry for the ages.

Thinking Window Verses was composed in Chinese characters, which the Han people brought to the Korean Peninsula in the first century B.C., along with Buddhism. Korean poets and writers adapted the Chinese characters to their own uses in a script that came to be known as Hanja, which was employed until the late nineteenth and early twentieth centuries. To translate *Thinking Window Verses*, then, it was first necessary for Professor Hyeonwu Lee to render the Hanja text into modern Korean, from which Professor Won-Chung Kim made a literal translation into English, and then I set to work trying to make these lines sing. The risk of a three-way translation project is that it may become a poetic version of the game of telephone, the form and content of the poems in English bearing little resemblance to the original. Hence the thousands of questions I posed to Professor Kim, my longtime translation partner, and the hundreds of footnotes included here, which serve as a gloss on Professor Hwan-kuk Jung's invaluable introduction to Kim Ryŏ and the challenges he faced—political, physical, and spiritual—with such equanimity.

"Out of life's school of war," Friedrich Nietzsche observed in *Twilight of the Idols*, "what doesn't kill me, makes me stronger." Exile can produce the same result, according to the Polish poet Czesław Miłosz, whose long exile in France and the United States shaped a body of work that rightly earned him the Nobel Prize for Literature. We hope that with this translation of *Thinking Window Verses* Kim Ryŏ will find his place in the vibrant tradition of exile literature in English.

Christopher Merrill
Director, International Writing Program
The University of Iowa

Introduction

1. Tamjŏng Kim Ryŏ and His Literary World

Tamjŏng Kim Ryŏ (1766-1822) is one of the most underrated writers in Korean literary history. In his time, Yŏnam Pak Chiwŏn, a master of classical literature and a representative Sirhak[1] scholar, and Tasan Chŏngyak Yong were the most esteemed writers. In the shadow of these literary giants, Kim was regarded as just "a minor writer at the border." His close friend Munmuja Yi Ok (1760-1815) has lately attracted notice, but Kim remains unknown, although he holds an important place in the literary renaissance of the late Chosŏn period. There are two reasons for his relatively low esteem: 1) many of his writings were lost during his exile, and 2) scholars have failed to discern the charm and meaning of Kim's work until now.

As a student in Sŏngkyunkwan, an exile, and a local administrator late in life, Kim was never in a position to wield political or social influence. His family belonged to the Patriarch Faction (Noron 老論), the central political power of the time, but he enjoyed no privileges from that. In short, his ambitions were thwarted in politics and literature alike. The world took no notice of him; most of

---

[1] Sirhak (also spelled Silhak) was a Korean Confucian social reform movement in the late Chosŏn period. *Sil* means "actual" or "practical," and *hak* means "studies" or "learning." It developed in response to the increasingly metaphysical nature of Neo-Confucianism (성리학), which seemed disconnected from the rapid agricultural, industrial, and political changes occurring in Korea between the late 17th and early 19th centuries.

his writings date from his time in exile.

In 1797, at the age of thirty-two, Kim was exiled for his alleged involvement in the criminal case of Kang Ich'ŏn, a close friend and classmate at Sŏngkyunkwan. It was reported that Kang had contacted Catholics and was spreading Catholicism, and Kim took part in this affair. King Chŏngjo was enforcing the rectification of literary style (*munch'e panjŏng* 文體反正), aiming to stop the harmful stylistic effects of popular essays on minor subjects (*sop'ummun*) and foster a revival of the classical elegant style. Its hidden purpose was to root out heretical Western ideas, particularly Catholicism. Kim and his friends at Sŏngkyunkwan, Yi Ok, Kang Ich'ŏn, and Kim Chosun, wrote in the style of essays on minor subjects, and while Yi was sentenced to serve in the military (from which noblemen were exempted) Kim received a verbal warning, and Kang, exiled to Cheju Island, was executed in the Catholic Persecution of 1801. Kim, charged with the crimes of being a *sop'ummun* writer and a Catholic, was exiled for ten years.

His exile led him to face his circumstances squarely and to learn from the real lives of common people in Chosŏn society, notably those he met in exile, whom he regarded as his equal. His experiences inspired two extraordinary books, *Thinking Window Verses* (*Sayuakpu*), which depicts his life in Puryŏng, and *Report on the Strange Fish of Chinhae* (*Wuhaeiŏbo*), an account of the various kinds of fish found in Wuhae, present-day Chinhae. Unlike other books about fish, which describe their shape and habits, Kim added heptasyllabic quatrains about the lives of the fishermen—a unique work in praise of the people and the sea.

Though Kim's work in exile constitutes the core of his writing, what he wrote after his liberation cannot be ignored. He lived in poverty until he secured a lowly governmental position. He cultivated a field, grew vegetables and fruit trees, and wrote poems about farming. *Ancient-style Poetry for Chang Wŏnkyŏng's Wife*, also known as *Song of Pangju*, is a long narrative poem whose date of composition is uncertain. Six hundred and eight couplets are preserved; half of the text did not survive. The poem celebrates the marriage of Pangju, a butcher's daughter in a remote area, to the son of a military officer. Though we cannot know the end of the story because of its missing lines, the marriage seems to have overcome the barrier of rank, revealing Kim's vision for a new society in which changes in social status and relationships between men and women regardless of rank might be possible.

2. Exile Literature and *Thinking Window Verses*

Thinking Window Verses, Kim Ryŏ's masterpiece, is the product of exile. Implicated in Kang Ich'ŏn's baseless rumor, he was exiled to Puryŏng, where he lived for five years. In 1802 his case was reexamined, and Kim was sent to Chinhae, Kyŏngsang Province, where he lived for five more years until he was freed. He wrote many books in exile, though most were lost, and thus he deserves to be called an exile writer.

Exile literature is a unique literary genre in traditional East-Asian society, especially in China and Korea, where many writers wrote much of their work in exile. Without exile literature, it is nearly impossible to discuss the history of literature in the late Chosŏn period. Tasan Chŏng Yakyong, one of the most famous Sirhak scholars, was exiled in Kangjin for 18 years during which he wrote *Admonitions on Governing the People* (*Mongmin simsŏ*). Exiling someone was viewed as a benevolent gesture in the

Chosŏn dynasty, when the king might have condemned him to death for his transgressions. Exile was designed to separate the sinner from political circles for a time.

It is no overstatement to say that exile was a fate that noblemen engaged in politics hoped to avoid. For the pain of exile was beyond description, and many died far from home. Ironically, exile offered writers who had no political ambition material for their work. Most exiles were noblemen from Seoul or high governmental officers, and now they could not help but experience directly the lives of commoners. In a hierarchical society, where the scope of their lives was limited by their social class, the new perspective they acquired at the far edges of the country allowed them to examine their political views and ideas about society.

That Kim Ryŏ was exiled twice, first to the northernmost Puryŏng, Hamgyŏng Province, and then to the southernmost Chinhae, Kyŏngsang Province, was unusual, and Kim was forced to live in two places whose climate and culture were dramatically different. But he fit in with the local people, becoming one with them—an exile who transcended the barriers of his social status. Unlike exiles who were miserable in these remote villages and patronized the locals, Kim did not look down on his new neighbors. He saw things from their point of view. *Thinking Window Verses* and *Report of Strange Fishes of Chinhae* grew out of his changed attitude toward them, the first singing of the northerners' tough spirit in the face of a harsh environment in Puryŏng, the second depicting the indigenous fish of Chinhae and lives of the fishermen.

3. The Contents and Characteristics of *Thinking Window Verses*

Kim wrote *Thinking Window Verses* in Chinhae, his second place of exile, missing Puryŏng and the people he had met there. This book contains three hundred poems composed over a lengthy period after his arrival in Chinhae in 1802. The poems are unique in form, each containing twelve phrases, unlike traditional Chinese poems, which usually take the form of a quatrain or regulated verses or couplets, and have either four, eight, or sixteen phrases. Kim's poems have twelve phrases, somewhere in the middle between regulated verse (eight phrases) and regulated couplets; furthermore, the first and second lines have five syllables apiece while the rest have seven. The form may be unconventional, but the first and second lines of every poem are the same: "I ask, what do you think / of our beloved northern seaside?" The poet supplies various answers in the following lines, inventing a form of call-and-response for the composition of poems in Chinese characters.

Kim's decision to write about his first place of exile while in Chinhae leads us to ask what his life was like in Puryŏng and why he poured such emotion into his poems. In his Preface to *Thinking Window Verses,* he explains: "One thinks when he is happy, and one does when sad. So how do I think? I think when I am standing, sitting, walking, and even lying down. Sometimes I think for a short while, other times at length. Sometimes the more I think, the harder it is to forget. My thinking stirs up feelings and sounds naturally follow. When I rhymed the sounds, a poem was written." In the 116th poem, Kim vividly describes what he could not forget:

> I lived in Puryŏng for only five years,
> but I think about it day and night.
> I'm going crazy longing for it;

THINKING WINDOW VERSES

my heart and bowels ache, as if cut apart.
Even in dream, my soul wanders about elderly Sŏ's house,
where I lived, south of Murŭng and west of Mt. Unryong.

Even in dreams, Kim revisits the house of Mr. Sŏ where he lived. He never stops thinking about Puryŏng and longs to return there. The title of the last section of this serial poem, "Though I Make up My Mind Not to Think," aptly summarizes his feelings for Puryŏng, which border on obsession. Who misses such a place? No one in that time missed their place of exile like Kim, and no one wrote three hundred poems about it with such feeling. This exile had a special affection for the people, produce, and ecology of Puryŏng.

4. The Narrative of Yŏnhŭi and Kim's Love for Her

Yŏnhŭi is the most frequently mentioned character in *Thinking Window Verses*, appearing in more than fifty poems. It is no exaggeration to say this book is for her. In the second poem Kim praises her figure, filial piety, the fine cloth she wove, and the advice she offers. He meets her often in his dreams. Seasonal festival days bring back memories of her—the January full moon ceremony (147), Dano Day (52), the wine she sent on the Double Ninth Festival (35), the red bean porridge she brought on the winter solstice (243). He thinks of her on her birthday, at the end of the rainy season, when the autumn leaves change colors, when snow falls, and when spring flowers open. Yŏnhŭi is the chief reason why Kim misses Puryŏng.

Who is Yŏnhŭi? A gisaeng in Puryŏng. Originally, gisaengs were lower-class women attached to a government office, professional singers and dancers who also did some chores. Yŏnhŭi must have been an official entertainer, and theirs is a meeting between an exile and a gisaeng in a remote region. Calling her "a fair Hang'a² of the north and spouse of a heavenly hermit," Kim does not hesitate to announce that he "got close to Yŏnhŭi in Puryŏng" (2). Their relationship transcends differences between a nobleman and a gisaeng, beyond the barriers of social status and position. Though Yŏnhŭi was a gisaeng at a distant border, she was a woman of higher aspirations with the free "spirit of a butterfly and the pure vital force of Mt. Changbaek" (12). She was also an excellent poet. She not only carefully prepared food and clothes for him but was a friend and partner who consoled and advised Kim. She warned him that his writing could ruin him and asked him to be cautious. Indeed he suffered severely for his writing. And he trusted her. Their relationship was more than an affair between a man and a woman. As we can see in "Staying up all night, wrapped in a cold comforter, / we talked about things old and new, wiping away our tears" (106); they were soulmates who shared the same fate.

Yŏnhŭi's story is preserved in Kim's poems. She might have been a forgotten gisaeng in the border region, but in *Thinking Window Verses* she lives on as a special woman. Kim lovingly describes her character, capacity, and spiritual world. It is said that he wrote another book, *Words and Deeds of Yŏnhŭi*, which was lost during his exile. Writing *The Words and Deeds of Someone* is impossible unless that person is worth following. Yŏnhŭi was such a person, at least to Kim.

---

² 姮娥, Heng'e: A fairy who lives on the moon in ancient Chinese mythology.

THINKING WINDOW VERSES

5. The Products and People of Puryŏng

Though Yŏnhŭi is a pivotal figure in *Thinking Window Verses*, she is not the only reason that Kim yearns for Puryŏng. He misses everything he experienced there—the landscape, food, and people merge into one, often delighting him. He recalls that "Rice grains are oily and millet smells fragrant. / Delicacies of the land are rich and the seafood is excellent" (145), and "Braised pheasant and venison jerky, the green onion kimchi from Musan" (20) were best accompanied by wine. The foods he enjoyed in Puryŏng, like marinated crabs, sweet rice balls, steamed corn, and melon, became the subjects of his poems.

  The natural world and produce of this northern area were unfamiliar to him, even exotic, and the freezing winter was hard to endure. To survive in such harsh circumstances, northerners used animal hides to make sheepskin overcoats and marten hats. He saw the sacred Oh dog, the silky fowl, a foal from Manchuria, a duck hawk, the charming cat, and a sparrow hawk, all of which eventually entered his poems. But even more attractive were the people he met. Saying "Even heartless mountains and rivers are like that, / my friends, no need to say anything" (298), he calls them out one by one. Some were men of letters, though Kim was attracted more to the strong, brave people of the area, including Hwang Taesŏk, who had no peer in riding horses, archery, and martial arts; Chi Tŏkhae, who was well-read in military science; and Yang Kiwi, who defeated more than one hundred Ch'ing merchants. Because politicians discriminated against the people in the area, serving as a military officer was the only way for them to secure a government post, though they were usually low-ranking officers. Many men of letters looked down on these tough brave people but Kim Ryŏ regarded them with respect and affection. He felt sorry for them not being recognized, trapped in this forgotten place, despite their talents: "Heaven gave birth to a man to use somewhere, / but why is he wasting his time in this backwater?" He celebrates Puryŏng in praise songs for the unyielding spirit of the border people in this harsh environment.

Juxtaposed to the good people stand wicked government officials, whom Kim does not hesitate to name and shame: "Okryŏn garrison clerk Ch'oe, a real rascal, brought calamity through his cunning tricks and mad deeds" (224) and "Hyŏnsong and Kyŏngsu are worthless men" (279). His fury at corrupt officials—"How can I get hold of the executioner's sword / to cut off this wicked man's head?"—is balanced by his regard for the people of Puryŏng who keep their spirits up despite the painful repression that evil officials impose on them. Kim portrays more than one hundred people, including a hermit, a Confucian scholar, a filial son, a widow, a virtuous woman, gisaengs, fishermen, merchants, and skilled doctors. In short, real life.

6. The Ecology of the Border Area in the Chosŏn Dynasty

Located at the northern end of the Korean peninsula, Puryŏng never figured in history beyond hosting exiles in the Chosŏn era until Kim foregrounded it in *Thinking Window Verses*, which depict every aspect of life in Puryŏng, including its people, politics, economy, and culture—a rare kind of poetry, which was not designed to be encyclopedic. Yet *Thinking Window Verses* portrays the place, people, and daily life in their entirety. Here is one notable example:

> When apricot flowers fall and millet buds sprout,

> trout swim toward the bend in the river.
> On a day of drizzle around the Chajangdam pond
> the water was deep, rocks were few, and the fish were fat.
> Village men came, clutching fish spears
> and scraped moss from the rocks together.
> The fisheyes that we boiled in an earthenware brazier were fresh,
> the color of makgeolli in the bowls and jars was beautiful. (51)

In this poem men spear fish, women cook fish soup in a kettle, and everyone drinks rice wine. Kim also invoked a women's outing to Hwajŏn, a spring picnic to the mountains to make pan-fried sweet rice cake decorated with flower petals, and women enjoying spring when azaleas open, eating flower pancakes and singing.

Thinking Window Verses is a fine example of ethnopoetics—and so much more.

Hwan-kuk Jung
Professor of Korean Language and Literature
Dongkuk University

Thinking Window Verses

Preface

"Thinking Window" (思牖) is the title of the framed picture hung from the right window of the house I have rented. When I was in the north, no day passed without me thinking of the south; now in the south no day passes without me thinking of the north. My thinking often changes like this, but my agony daily worsens. This is why I framed the window. I copied a poem by Jia Langxian[3] on a clean sheet of paper and pasted it to my window:

> Ten years have passed at the guest house in Bingzhou,
> Day and night my heart was eager to return to my home in Xianyang.
> After crossing the Sanggan River again for no reason,
> I look at Bingzhou and think it may be my hometown.

I think of the north in roughly the same way. One thinks when one is happy and sad. So how do I think? I think when I am standing, sitting, walking, even lying down. Sometimes I think in a short burst, other times at length. Sometimes the more I think, the harder it is to forget. My thinking stirs up feelings in my heart, and sounds naturally follow. When I rhymed the sounds, a poem was written.

These poems are unsuited for musical performance, being vulgar and unrefined. But compared to the songs of

---

[3] Jia Dao (賈島). His penname was Langxian (浪仙). He was a Chinese Buddhist monk and poet active during the Tang dynasty. The title of the poem is "Crossing Sanggan" (渡桑乾)

Wu(吳) and Cai(蔡),[4] they reflect my own thinking in my own style. Therefore, I wrote down some of the poems and named them *Thinking Window Verses*.

December 15, 1801. An exile Tamwôn[5] writes.

---

[4] Countries in the Spring and Autumn Waring States period
[5] Kim Ryŏ's penname.

KIM RYŎ

1. *Old Man Ch'a*

I ask, what do you think
of our beloved northern seaside?
Mr. Ch'a of Ch'ŏngam is a nine-ch'ŏk[6] tall old man
whose hair and beard have turned white.
In his prime, he says, he liked to travel
and roamed around the eight provinces[7] on horseback.
He returned home after spending his fortune
and plows his rocky fields, living like a hermit in a thatched house.
Even at the age of fifty, he likes to read books,
light a lamp, and stay up all night.
He keeps a hundred books of *The Collected Works of Chu Hsi* handy
and reads them over and over until they turn to fluff.

Ch'ŏngam is a placename. Mr. Cha's given name is Namgyu, his other name is Yŏyong, and he was a student of Yi Manjang. He is a descendant of Cha Tŭkto, a patriot in the Japanese Invasion of Korea in 1592.

---

[6] Traditional Korean measure of length. One ch'ŏk is about 30.3 cm.
[7] The territory of Korea, which was divided into eight provinces.

THINKING WINDOW VERSES

2. *Yŏnhŭi*[8]

I ask, what do you think
of our beloved northern seaside?
I got close to Yŏnhŭi at Puryŏng,
a fair Hang'a[9] of the north and spouse of a heavenly hermit.
She had the spirit of snow and ice, a jade-like figure
with red lips, white teeth, dark eyebrows.
Her raven black hair fluttered like a cloud,
her fingers were white like onion roots, her skin glossy.
She was glamorous, noble-minded, calm;
like mountains and rivers, she was loving and amicable.
She was clear and pleasant, neat and polite,
and her demeanor was natural and easy in every aspect.

Yŏnhŭi's family name is Chi, her name is Yŏnhwa, her other name is Ch'unsim, and her penname is Hahŏn. She was the keeper of the Ch'ŏnyŏngnu Pavilion. I wrote The Chronicle of Yŏnhŭi's Sayings and Doings *separately.*

---

[8] Her name means "A Lotus Woman."
[9] 姮娥, Heng'e: A fairy who lives on the moon in ancient Chinese mythology.

3. *The Taste of Pujang[10] Hwang's Rice Wine*

I ask, what do you think
of our beloved northern seaside?
Outside the Western Gate, to the right of the Southern Stream,
lies the house of Pujang Hwang, whose wine is said to be the best.
This wine fermented from clean millet[11] and pressed proso millet
fills more than a hundred mal[12] of earthenware jars.
Mixed with pearl-shaped dewdrops of the dawn, this wine is agate red
and smells of turmeric, with an amber hue.[13]
The young woman by the furnace counts money
under the glowing lamp and boasts about the wine.
I, a scholar, like to get drunk with a beautiful woman
when the apricots blossom, but I cannot find myself there.

Pujang Hwang's given name is Sanch'un. His elder brother is Chigukwan[14] Hwang Ryun. Sanch'un lives outside the West Gate of the Puch'un Fortress, and his wife makes good wine.

---

[10] 部將: The sixth-ranked military officer in the *Five Commands*, in charge of a Pu of twenty-five soldiers. Pujang Hwang was a military official without rank, having failed the state exam.
[11] This phrase comes from Du Fu's "憶昔 Recalling the Past": "Unglutinous rice is rich and millet is sweet."
[12] Korean unit of measure. One mal is about eighteen liters.
[13] The phrase comes from Li Bai's "客中行 Guest in the Line": "Lanling wine is brewed of turmeric, the amber light is crystal clear in the jade bowl.
[14] 知穀官: A military official assigned to a provincial camp.

4. *Yŏnhŭi's House*

I ask, what do you think
of our beloved northern seaside?
The street east of the fortress is still vivid in my memory.
Yŏnhŭi lives by the second bridge on that street.
A clear stream flows in front of her house
and rugged rocks loom around the mountain.
Dozens of willows grow in the valley,
the one outside her door reflecting on the pavilion.
Her loom is set by the window on the pavilion,
a small stone mortar sits under the pavilion.
A cherry tree grows by the well south of the pavilion,
the road to Hoeryŏng[15] stretches north, beyond the pavilion.

---

[15] The northernmost town of Hamgyŏng Province, located on the border with Manchuria. A market has been held there to trade with the Qing since the time of King Injo.

5. *Kim Hŭiik, a Talented Man*

I ask, what do you think
of our beloved northern seaside?
There is a talented man in Puryŏng whose other name is
    Hŭiik,
with clear and handsome eyebrows shining bright as a
    picture.
His mind is like the autumn moon reflected in an ice jar,[16]
the red jade-like words coming from his mouth surprise
    people.
Like fragrant plants and beautiful trees in the garden of the
    Sa family,[17]
his taste for art and beautiful colors is blossoming now.
Swift and sturdy, he moves like the heavenly horse from
    Akwa[18]
that gallops with a fierce spirit, spouting blood and sweat.
As a saint appears when the Hwangha River clears once in
    a thousand years,[19]

---

[16] An ice jar (冰壺) is a jade jar in which to keep ice, used here to describe the character of Lǐ Dòng (李侗), Zhu Xi's (朱熹) teacher. "The autumn moon reflected in an ice jar" means a clear, high mind free of any taint.

[17] 謝 Xie: The garden of the Xie family was a metaphor for excellent children. The phrase came from an old story. When Xie An (謝安) asked, "Why do people want to have outstanding children?," his nephew Xiexuan replied, "To use a metaphor, it's like people wanting fragrant plants and beautiful trees to grow in their garden."

[18] 渥洼 Wowa: The word for water in Anxixian, Ganssisheng. Emperor Wu of the Han dynasty found a heavenly horse in this water.

[19] The Huanghe River: The water of the Huanghe River is murky,

so you should work hard to get out into the world.

My student, Kim Hyŏngyu, uses Hŭiik as his other name. He is the talented son of a famous family in Puryŏng.

---

but once in a thousand years it clears. When this happens, it is regarded as a sign that a saint will be born.

6. *The Moon at the Yŏngnak Pavilion*

I ask, what do you think
of our beloved northern seaside?
How many people climbed the Yŏngnak Pavilion today
to enjoy the bright moon rising by the eaves?
I still remember the May night last year
when the crescent moon appeared at the edge
of the pavilion. Silently, I climbed alone
to sing and chant, gazing down at the blue pond.
The moonlight is constant year after year,
but my life is wretched, I wander like mugwort.
An exile's life in the south and north is endless pain.
I don't know yet whether I will head east or west next year.

Built by the former governor, Han Ŭnggŏm, the pavilion was located hundreds of steps south of the fortress. Under the pavilion were white rocks and a clear stream. The forest was dense and the trees were tall.

THINKING WINDOW VERSES

7. *Kang Ŭngya*

I ask, what do you think
of our beloved northern seaside?
I dearly loved Kang Ŭngya from Eastern village.
With a fine, generous figure, he was elegant and modest.
This son of jade planted in Namjŏn[20]—
how can we compare his worth to Yŏnsŏk?[21]
With his prudent spirit and the clear mind of a government vessel,
he is destined to become either Horyŏn[22] or Yŏbon.[23]
Besides, he was learned in all things, well read;
his plump belly is the bookcase of the *Five Classics*.[24]
An inchworm crawls only to unfurl its wings later.
Someday he will beat his wings and fly ten thousand miles like a roc.

---

[20] 藍田 Nantian: A place known to produce high-quality jade. For his virtuous deeds Yang Boyong received 180 liters of stone seed from a heavenly being, which he sowed in Nantian; all grew into jade: a metaphor for good children worthy of excellent parents.
[21] 燕石 Yanshi: A stone resembling jade, which is produced in Yanshan and used as a metaphor for worthless things.
[22] 瑚璉 Hulian: Utensils used in a royal ancestral rite; a metaphor for a talented man who can complete a large mission.
[23] 璵璠 Yubo: High-quality jade used as a metaphor for a virtuous, respectable person.
[24] The *Five Classics* consisting of the *Book of Odes*, *Book of Documents*, *Book of Changes*, *Book of Rites*, and *The Spring and Autumn Annals*.

Kang Ŭngya's name is Sangguk. His learning was deep, his actions, pure. I taught him The Collected Works of Chu Hsi (朱書) *and* Jinsilu (近思錄).

THINKING WINDOW VERSES

8. *Red Cherry*

I ask, what do you think
of our beloved northern seaside?
The tree by the well bore ten thousand cherries,
the long and short boughs sagged.
Yŏnhŭi picked cherries and put them in a basket,
each one round and bright as a crystal.
She gripped one and bit, saying,
"Which is redder, my lips or the cherry?"
For three years, when this old man was exiled to the rough border,
I filled my hungry stomach with cherries.
Today I see flowers on the tree.
After blossoming, its fruit will ripen at the right time.

A cherry tree was growing by the well south of Yŏnhŭi's tower. The tree was originally from Yŏnggot'ap.[25] The fruit was the size of a cow's eyeball, and tasted sweet and delicious. It is called "cow's eyeball cherry."

---

[25] 寧古塔 Ningguta: The place where the Qing dynasty originated, comprising the area around Ninghe District in Heilongjian Province.

9. *Mr. Nam's Son*

I ask, what do you think
of our beloved northern seaside?
Seven or eight youths seem to have a promising future,
though the talent of Mr. Nam's son is truly extraordinary.
Carefully folding papers made in Yongyŏn,[26]
he draws big stokes, which bring forth ripples.
If he strips some flesh and adds some bones to his writing,
his calligraphy will easily surpass that of Hongjŏnja.[27]
Modest and upright, he acts like he is deaf,
but proves heroic when he gets drunk.
I miss you, I'm sad not to see you.
I gaze at the distant sky, worrying.

The student Nam's name is Hŭngyu; his other name is Konso. Yongyŏn is the name of a temple. Hongjŏnja refers to Shin Wi, who is a skilled modern calligrapher.

---

[26] When government-run paper shops declined in the late Chŏsun dynasty, temples that retained paper-making skills became the main suppliers of paper.

[27] The penname of Shin Wi (1769-1845); Chaha and Kyôngsudang are his other pennames. One of the best poets of the Chŏsun dynasty and an excellent calligrapher, he was widely known in China. He is the author of *The Complete Works of Kyôngsudang*. *The Poetical Works of Chaha* (edited by Kim Taekyông) contains six hundred poems by Shin.

10. *Pak Han'gi*

I ask, what do you think
of our beloved northern seaside?
Pak Han'gi, living in Kujŏngch'ŏn,
descends from generations of upright nobility.
He keeps the seven books of *Mencius*[28] on his desk,
muttering and memorizing them day and night.
To read well means to understand something in detail.
One does not need to read five carts of books on many
    topics.[29]
Taking pity on me for living alone, friendless,
he visits me daily, stopping by my wormwood-covered gate.
He braved yesterday's rain and came again today in rain.
The muddy autumn road doesn't hinder him.

Kujŏngch'ŏn is a placename. Pak Han'gi's name is Chinnam. His father Honggyu is the Chehal[30] of Puryŏng.

---

[28] 孟子 Mencius, the saint of Zhou (named after his hometown), is regarded in Confucianism as the second most important figure after Confucius. *The Mencius* is composed of seven books.
[29] The five carts of books mean extensive knowledge. The phrase comes from *Zhuang Zhou*: "Huishi's theory is extensive and his books amount to five carts."
[30] A petty local officer in charge of personnel and resources.

11. Brave Ach'o[31] Ch'a

I ask, what do you think
of our beloved northern seaside?
There were two hundred civilian houses inside the fortress,
and Ach'o Ch'a was strong as a tiger.
When a gelded black ox ran amok at the fortress gate,
he stopped it with one hand.
When the mad cow hit him in the balls and split open his sack,
he sewed it back together with a twist of horsehair.
Ach'o Ch'a was a good friend
who came to see me whenever there was wine in the jar.
He boasted of loading his bow with iron triggers[32]
and flying into the road right after sewing up his balls.

Ach'o Ch'a's name is Ijin, and his other name is Tongsuk. He is a descendant of Tŏkhong,[33] a younger cousin of Ch'a Tŭkto, and his grandfather is Manung. I wrote the epigraph for Tŏkhong and The Life of Ch'a Manung *separately.*

---

[31] Abyŏng was a soldier who served the general at headquarters, and Ach'o was a soldier in charge of the guards.
[32] A bow with iron triggers that can shoot many arrows, one after another.
[33] Cha Tŏkhong passed the military examination during King Sŏnjo's reign and was appointed myriarch. He and his older cousin Ch'a Tŭkto were killed in the Imjin War.

THINKING WINDOW VERSES

12. *Poems of Yŏnhŭi*

I ask, what do you think
of our beloved northern seaside?
There are scores of famous writers in our country
and Hagok's sister[34] is the best of the poets.
Yŏnhŭi's poems are comparable to those of Wikang[35]
and much better than those of T'ak Mungun[36] or Wang
   Chang.[37]
Yŏnhŭi has the mind of a parrot and spirit of a butterfly,
snow-white features and a heart of silk.
The pure vital force of Mt. Changbaek

---

[34] Hŏ Ch'ohŭi (1563-1589), a female poet in the middle Chŏsun period, wrote poems from the age of eight, though in her will she dictated that her work should be confiscated upon her death. Her brother, Hŏ Kyun, gave some of her poems to Zhu Zhiffn, who published them to acclaim in China. The book also appeared in Japan in 1711.

[35] 衛姜 Wei Jiang, aka Zhuang Jiang, wife of Duke Zhuang of Wey in the Spring and Autumn period, is regarded as China's greatest female poet. She wrote the first five poems in *The Book of Odes,* 燕燕, Yanyan), 終風, Zhongfeng), 柏舟, Bozhou), 녹의(綠衣, Luxi), and 일월(日月, Riyue).

[36] 卓文君 Zhuo Wenjun (fl. 2nd century BC): A poet in the **Western Han** dynasty. As a young widow, she eloped with the poet **Sima Xiangru**. "Baitou Yin" (白頭吟, Song of White Hair), which laments the inconstancy of male love, is attributed to her.

[37] 王嫱 Wang Qiang (also 王檣 and 王牆), commonly known by her stylistic name 王昭君 Wang Zhaojun, was one of ancient China's **Four Beauties**. She was born in the Western Han dynasty, in Baoping Village in **Hubei Province**, and was sent by **Emperor Yuan** to marry **Xiongnu Chanyu Huhanye** (呼韓邪) to foster friendly relations with the Han dynasty.

has produced a flower bud over two thousand years.
Yŏnhŭi, Yŏnhŭi, you must be the fairy of heaven.
Why are you buried in this secluded border region?

Hagok Hŏbong's sister was Ch'ohŭi; her other name was Kyŏngbŏn and her penname was Nansŏlhŏn. She was a fine poet whose collected works remain in print. Mt. Changbaek is the tallest mountain in Kwanbuk Province.

THINKING WINDOW VERSES

13. *Puryŏng Swallow*

I ask, what do you think
of our beloved northern seaside?
A pair of swallows used to fly in and out of my house,
returning every year for our reunion.
The hair on the back of an old exile in a southern town has turned grey,
moss has grown in the yard, dust is thick on my bed.
The twig gate is closed tight. No visitors:
only swallows arriving regularly to keep me company.
What's the use of talking about the unpredictability of the world?
Exceeding all expectations, I am eating my meals in Chinhae.
I meet southern swallows instead of northern ones.
I swallow my tears, I wander, I sigh in vain.

When I rented a house in exile in Puryŏng, a pair of white-headed swallows built a nest on the doorpost, returning every year. I wrote The Story of White-headed Swallows *separately.*

14. *A Pear Tree and an Apricot Tree*

I ask, what do you think
of our beloved northern seaside?
A green ox mill and patterned bricks encircled the well.
South of the well stood a red pear tree behind an apricot tree.
Yŏnhŭi planted the pear tree years before,
and I planted an apricot tree last year.
The pear tree bore fruit and the apricot bloomed;
the fruit was tinged with red like her lips and the flowers were like her ruddy cheeks.
When I stood by the pear tree, it rose above my forehead,
and when Yŏnhŭi stood by the apricot tree, it reached her shoulders.
This is what a separation is like in the human world.
How can careless trees know sorrow?

There was an empty lot south of the well, where Yŏnhŭi planted a Yŏnji pear tree[38] and a red apricot tree. Last year the pear tree bore fruit and the apricot bloomed for the first time.

---

[38] Yŏnji is a slope on Mt. Ch'ŏnggye in Puryŏng. A note to #66 reads, "Mt. Ch'ŏnggye is thirty li east of town. The slope is called Yŏnji, because Yŏnji pear trees grow there."

15. *The Dog I Raised*

I ask, what do you think
of our beloved northern seaside?
At a Chinese store in Kyŏngwŏn last year
someone from Palgat'oe was selling a white long-mouthed dog:
"This is a breed of sacred Oh[39] from Yŏnggot'ap.[40]
He is smart and brave and quick, as if he moves with flying feet."
I reared him for a few months, and he slept under my bed,
with frost-white hair covering his temple and his ears pricked.
When the Commander of the State Tribunal[41] came,
the dog cried suddenly, burrowed into my knees,
then ran away like an arrow, disappearing to the north.
I lost him, looked in vain toward the cold northern mountains.

---

[39] 神獒 Shen ao: A sacred dog, Ao. Ao is the Chinese name for a mastiff.

[40] Palgat'oe (勃哥堆 Bogedui) and Yŏunggot'ap (寧古塔 Ningguta) are places in Manchuria.

[41] Kŭmorang (金吾郎): The Commander of the State Tribunal. Kim Ryŏ was transferred from Puryŏng to the Seoul State Tribunal in March 1801, accused of associating with the Catholic Kang Ich'ŏn. The Chosŏn government had rejected Catholicism, and Catholic believers were persecuted for fear they would disturb a regime based on Confucianism.

Kyŏngwŏn Tohobu[42] *is located three hundred li north of Puryŏng Fortress. Chinese people in the Qing dynasty opened a market there. Palgat'oe and Yŏnggot'ap are placenames for Oh's homes.*

---

[42] 慶源都護府: **Kyŏngwŏn** regional military command.

16. *A Couple of Black Silkies*[43]

I ask, what do you think
of our beloved northern seaside?
Last year Mr. Chang, chief peddler of Yŏnch'ŏn,
gave me a pair of black silkies for a present.
Their skin was raven black, their feathers white as snow,
and the red spot in their breast shone like moonlight.
Nor did they fail to wake an exile from his sleep,
crying cock-a-doodle-doo deep into the night.
All the thirty eggs they laid in spring
hatched into chicks and grew into goslings.
I cut down trees and built fences in vain.
Who knew that wildcats and weasels[44] would run rampant?

Yŏnch'ŏn is a placename. Chief Chang's name is Chŏngse; his other name is Paeksang.

---

[43] A breed of chicken with black skin and bones, called Ogolgye (烏骨鷄) in Korean.

[44] The original meaning of "a flying squirrel" is inadequate, so it is translated as "weasel."

17. Yi Kwangsa[45] and His Son[46]

I ask, what do you think
of our beloved northern seaside?
Tobo's calligraphy is like Wang Hŭiji's,[47]
Yŏngik's writings can compete with Sajo's.[48]
They are the son and father of Pegasus and the phoenix;
they won't stand below So Tongp'a brothers on Mt. Ami.[49]
Though Yŏngik has great talent,
both live in exile at the northern border.
The misfortune of a man of letters:
It's all over when he falls.
Drunk, I think of the past, weeping by the river;
the desolate autumn wind rises in the tall tree.

---

[45] 李匡師 Yi Kwangsa (1705-178): A writer and calligrapher in the late Chosŏn period. His other name was Tobo, his pennames were Wŏnkyo and Subuk. He forged his own style of calligraphy called Wŏnkyo Style and published *The Collected Works of Wŏnkyo* and *The Essentials of Wŏnkyo*.

[46] 李令翊 Yi Yŏngik (1740-1780): A writer and calligrapher in the late Chosŏn period. His other names were Yugong and Inbo; his pennames were Sinjae and Manjang. He wrote *Works of Sinjae*.

[47] 王羲之 Wang Xizhi: A famous Chinese calligrapher. Yixiao was his other name.

[48] 謝朓 Xietiao: A landscape poet from Qi (齊) in the Nanchao (南朝) period.

[49] Refers to the Su brothers, Sudongpo (蘇東波) and Suzhe (蘇轍), who were from Mt. Emei in Sichuansheng. Along with their father, Suxun (蘇洵), they were among the eight greatest writers of the Song and Tang dynasties.

THINKING WINDOW VERSES

In 1755, during the reign of King Yŏngjo, Tobo Yi Kwangsa and his son Inbo Yŏngik were exiled to Puryŏng. Their relics are scattered around the town.[50]

---

[50] Yi Kwangsa lived in Puryŏng for seven years. He devoted himself to studying and calligraphy, gathering many disciples. This brought him misfortune. A memorial to the king was delivered to the Office of the Inspector-General in 1762 ordering Yi to be re-exiled to an isolated island, because as a sinner he incited others through his teachings. Chuae, the daughter he begot in Puryŏng, was said to be unsurpassed level in calligraphy.

18. Sŭng[51] Pak

I ask, what do you think
of our beloved northern seaside?
Pak's fidelity is clear as ice, firm as stone,
pure as frost. Who can sully it?
In honesty he is equal to Ch'och'ŏnji,[52]
and he is more meticulous than Yut'akchi.[53]
What's more, he remains upright in the face of evil;
his appearance is extraordinary, like an eagle in the autumn sky.
There isn't much to do in a small town,
but he always has his ledgers and even stays up through the night.
Because cunning petty officials shudder and local strongmen lie low,
Commander Yi has nothing to do but whistle at his leisure.

Sŭng Pak's name is Hongjung; his other name is Paegŭi. He is a sixth-generation descendent of Martyr Pak Inbŏm,[54] who was killed during the 1592 Japanese invasion of Chosŏn. Commander Yi's name is Ch'angbae.

---

[51] Sŭng (丞) was a petty provincial official.
[52] 焦千之 Jiaoqianzhi: A scholar of BeiSong (北宋), renowned for his exemplary behavior.
[53] 劉度支 Liuduzhi: Liu Yan(劉晏), a statesman and meticulous financier in the Tang dynasty.
[54] He passed the military examination during King Sŏnjo's reign; fought in the 1592 Japanese Invasion of Chosŏn under Commander Wŏnhŭi of Puryŏng and was killed in Immyŏng.

19. *The Artistic Taste of Paengnŭng*

I ask, what do you think
of our beloved northern seaside?
A thousand willow boughs sway beside the spring waters.
Paengnŭng's artistic taste recalls Changsŏ[55] of old.
He recited Cho Maengdŏk's "Kalsŏk Poems"[56] in the morning,
and cherished "Sajayŏn" singing about Namch'ung's[57] humble girl.
A thousand kŭn[58] of pork and a hundred jars of alcohol—
when he was tipsy, he would stare at the blue sky.
He looked great, with his black hair and red cheeks;
his boyish appearance excited everyone.
Two years have passed since I last saw this friend.
I gaze at the northern clouds and ask about him.

My student Chang Wŏnhong's other name is Paengnŭng.

---

[55] 張緒 Zhangxu: A man of Nanqi (南齊) celebrated for his noble poverty and purity.

[56] The other name of Cho Mengde (曺孟德) was Cao Cao (曺操), a politician in Houhan (後漢). His masterpiece, *Kalsŏk* (碣石 *Jieshi*) *Poems*, praises the large spirit of the universe.

[57] 謝自然 Xieziran: A poor woman from Nanchong (南充) who became a fairy after learning Taoist magic. Hanyu (韓愈), a noted Tang dynasty poet, wrote a poem based on this story.

[58] Kŭn is a Korean unit of weight, about six hundred g (1.323 lbs).

20. At Chang Kukpo's House

I ask, what do you think
of our beloved northern seaside?
When the snow stopped and the moon was bright as the
 sun at noon,
I went over to Chang Kukpo's house late one night.
In the warm room the sweet scent lingered on the folding
 screen;
a green Mongolian carpet was spread on the cattail mat.
A pretty gisaeng offered drinks in a feather-shaped glass.
The host lit a candle and held me tight.
I was served braised pheasant and venison jerky;
the green onion kimchi from Musan was white and sour.
We drank enough that day to stay happy for a thousand
 years.
We sat up all night and sang at the top of our lungs.

Chang Kukpo's name is Ch'ungbo, and he is a petty functionary in the regional military garrison. One snowy night last winter at his house, I drank with clerks from the provincial censor, Pak Kyŏngsil, and his companions. Musan produces green onions.

THINKING WINDOW VERSES

21. *Sŭng Pak Came to See Me*

I ask, what do you think
of our beloved northern seaside?
What remains vivid to me is the water flowing so high
in last fall's flood that you could not distinguish between
the trees and the stream.
Moss grew thick, my wooden shoes stuck in the mud,
wormwood flourished.
For ten days I lay in bed suffering from malaria.
Sŭng Pak came to see me,
and the red makgeolli[59] he brought was fragrant.
The affairs of men are like floating duckweed, meeting and
separating.
You went to an eastern county, and I was exiled to the
south.
Cut off from news of my old mother and sick wife,
I sigh only at twilight in a strange place.

Sŭng Pak Hongjung was caught last winter by the chief border inspector, Yi Pyŏngjŏng,[60] flogged, and banished to Anbyŏn. The regional military commander, Yi Ch'angbae, was also dismissed from his position and went back home.

---

[59] Traditional unstrained rice wine.
[60] 李秉鼎 (1742~1804): He passed the national military examination in 1766 and was Mayor of Hanyang (Seoul), Deputy Director of the Office of Special Advisers, Provincial Governor of Hamgyŏng Province, and Minister of Personnel. According to the official record compiled after his death, he "followed after men of power, pursed his interests, and was greedy." The official historian called the author of *Collected Works of Iam* "a talented writer."

22. Yŏnhŭi in Last Night's Dream

I ask, what do you think
of our beloved northern seaside?
In a dream last night I went to Yŏnhŭi's house
and talked of the past, holding her hands.
She washed a glass, poured red wine
from the lacquered vat, and offered me a drink.
The scent of wild honey from Tonggwan was strong and thick,
the dried crab meat from Kijin was clean and light.
When I pointed at the fabric spread on the fulling block between the windows,
she said it was light-pink silk with a crease pattern.
"I bought twenty cha[61] of it at Ch'ŏngsae
to sew a chŏksam[62] for my beloved and a chŏgori[63] for me."

Yŏnhŭi learned to make wine from wild grapes, excellent in color and taste. Tonggwan is a military post and producer of wild honey. Kijin is located at the bend in the sea in Puryŏng County.

---

[61] Cha is a traditional measure of length, about one foot.
[62] An unlined summer jacket.
[63] Traditional Korean jacket.

THINKING WINDOW VERSES

23. *The Chrysanthemums I Planted in the Yard*

I ask, what do you think
of our beloved northern seaside?
Bunches of chrysanthemums in the yard of the house I rented
blossomed red, white, purple, and yellow with a strong fragrance.
Wrongly thinking the plum rain [64] would be rare this summer,
I plowed some furrows and planted seedlings.
I plucked and ate the soft shoots
and brewed the flowers to pour into a gourd dipper.
Some people are fated to chew chrysanthemums.[65]
For no reason I walked again into the land of Yŏngnam.[66]
When I touch my belly and smell the fragrance on the wind,
the autumn clouds are desolate, and the year ends.

---

[64] Because the rainy season usually begins when plums mellow, it is called plum rain. Plums turn yellow in May.
[65] A metaphor for an exile's life. See Qu Yuan's poem, "Lisao": "I taste dew on orchids in the morning and fallen autumn chrysanthemums in the evening."
[66] The southeastern province of Korea. Chinhae, Kim's second place of exile, is located at the southern end of this province.

KIM RYŎ

24. *The Foal from Manchuria*

I ask, what do you think
of our beloved northern seaside?
My servant Wi went to the Chongsŏng market last winter
and bought a Manchurian foal for a hundred nyang.[67]
He was only six ch'ŏk[68] tall, pale yellow.
He had extraordinary mettle, and he ran like the devil.
His hair was like cut lemon silk, he had pricked ears,
his eyes sparked flames, and the pupils were rectangular.
There are many horses in the stable of the public office
but none can compare to this one.
I am here at present—my servant never returned there.
My poor horse, alas, must be rolling in the mud.

Chongsŏng Pu is 240 li from Puryŏng Fortress. Every year Chinese people stayed in Chongsŏng on their way home from trading their wares at Hoeryŏng.

---

[67] Nyang is a unit of old Korean coinage, its value varying.
[68] A traditional Korean unit of measure, about one foot.

25. *Ginseng*

I ask, what do you think
of our beloved northern seaside?
The owner of my house grew dozens of jars of ginseng,
planting a long cedar fence in deep holes,
which he covered with mounds of red clay and a layer of
 birch bark
so they would grow well with or without rain.
Locals called the ginseng flower "the moon,"
and they would visit to see "the moon" when it opened
 around Dano.[69]
I heard that ginseng is divine medicine,
with three forked branches and five shiny leaves.
Nangwŏn and Hyŏnp'o,[70] homes to the fairies, are not far
 away,
but why have I alone ended up in this desolate place?

*The owner of my rented house, Sŏ Myŏngwŏn,[71] had a field of
ginseng.*

---

[69] The fifth day of the fifth month of the year on the lunar calendar.

[70] 閬苑 Langyuan is the home of fairies atop Mt. Kunlun (崑崙). 玄圃 Xuanpu is another name for Langyuan.

[71] He seems to be in charge of watching Kim Ryŏ. The governor or local magistrate appointed someone to provide an exile with a room and to keep an eye on him.

26. *Hunter Ch'oe*

I ask, what do you think
of our beloved northern seaside?
Chigu[72] Ch'oe is stout, but quick and brave.
Sharp-eyed, swifter than a lynx,
he has been a skilled marksman since childhood.
He hiked around Nam Mountain to trap bears.
When an angry bear bit his forearm,
he stuck his gun in its mouth and shot it dead.
Last fall, when he came across a white-browed tiger in a valley,
he ripped open its belly with a single shot.
Ah, Ch'oe is a great hunter indeed!
He doesn't stoop to shooting roe deer in the forest.[73]

Ch'oe P'ok, a man from our town, was a master marksman. When a tiger came down into our village, he shot it dead. I wrote A Story of Ch'oe, a Master Hunter *separately.*

---

[72] 知彀: An official in the Military Training Office.
[73] The original is a python, but in this context it is translated as a roe deer.

27. Yŏnhŭi, a Noble Woman Warrior

I ask, what do you think
of our beloved northern seaside?
My heart is like steel tempered a hundred times
so that it will not break easily.
Even if I die, I will never forget Soryŏn
not for any grudge for her but for her kindness.
She is a noble warrior like Aba Kosaeng:[74]
her heroic spirit in helping me at an impasse reaches the sky.
Historically, there have been female noble warriors.
Sŏbaeng[75] of Simjŏngni must be one.
How can I borrow Yongmun Taesa's[76] brush
to highlight her name in history?

Soryŏn is Yŏnhŭi's childhood name.

---

[74] 古生 Gu Sheng: A character in Xue Tiao's novel 無雙傳, *Double Pass* 押牙. As a military official in charge of rituals and parades, she risked all to unite hero and heroine, taking his life so as not to cause trouble in the future.

[75] 聶榮 Nie Wei was 聶政 Nie Zheng's sister, and they were noble warriors in Sima Qian (司馬遷)'s *Shiji* (史記).

[76] 龍門太史 refers to Taishigong (太史公) Sima Qian (司馬遷).

KIM RYŎ

28. *A Mat from Tanch'ŏn*[77]

I ask, what do you think
of our beloved northern seaside?
Student Pak from Sŏam rode to my house
to give me a nice reed mat from Tanch'ŏn.
It was smooth as ice, clean as silver,
with a shining, radiant pattern.
When I spread it on the floor and lay down, even my bones
    felt clean.
It was better than a cattail mat, comparable to a silk rug.
I took care of it, treasured it,
and rolled it up to store when the weather turned cold.
How I miss it here, where the sun blazes
and soy-like sweat streams down.

Student Pak's name is Ŭijung; his other name is Chunghong. He is the brother of Hongjung and works as a librarian in Puryŏng Hyanggyo.[78]

---

[77] Tanch'ŏn is a town south of Puryŏng.
[78] Local Confucian schools in Koryŏ and Chosŏn.

THINKING WINDOW VERSES

29. *Medicinal Herbs Mr. Kim Sent Me*

I ask, what do you think
of our beloved northern seaside?
Worried about my health, Mr. Kim from east of town
sent his servant to me with a letter and medicine.
Tugu,[79] which protects the intestines, was hot and fragrant,
Pachyma was white as snow, and Chimo[80] was cool.
Also threads of gold to cleanse my heart,
choice products from Nagasaki and Chikuzen,[81]
and a few other herbs, all of which I took
and, magically, made a full recovery.
Now I suffer from hemoptysis, I'm chilled,
I toss and turn all night, gazing northward.

Hŭiik worried about my health and frequently sent me medicinal herbs.

---

[79] 荳蔲: An herbal medicine. Its scientific name is *Alpinia katsumadai* Hayata.
[80] 知母: An herbal medicine. Its scientific name is *Anemarrhena asphodeloides* Bunge.
[81] The old name for a town southwest of Fukuoka.

30. *The Fidelity of Kim Chekyŏm's Family*

I ask, what do you think
of our beloved northern seaside?
Disappointed, no one dares to speak about the Sinim Massacre;[82]
only the village elders tell Kim Chukch'wi's[83] story.
He was the son of Lord Ch'unghŏn[84] and grandson of Lord Munch'ung,[85]
a family renowned for its wisdom, integrity, and hidden virtues.
Four generations of the family were put to death for the king;

---

[82] Refers to a massacre in 1721-1722. When the four great men of the Patriach's Faction installed King Kyŏngjong's brother, Prince Yŏning, as Crown Prince and let him rule the country, the Disciple's Faction sent a memorial to the King accusing them of treason. The four minsters and other followers were either executed or exiled to the remotest borders.

[83] Kim Chekyŏm (1680-1722); Chukch'wi was his penname. A literary man in the late Chosŏn period. When his father Kim Ch'angjip was poisoned in 1722 by the Disciple's Faction, including Kim Ilkyŏng, he was exiled to Ulsan and later to Puryŏng, also to be poisoned to death.

[84] Kim Ch'angjip (1648-1722): Ch'unghŏn is his posthumous title. A literary man in the late Chosŏn period, and one of the so-called four ministers of the Patriach's Faction, he was thorn hedged in a house in Kŏjedo Island in the 1722 massacre and poisoned to death in Sŏngju.

[85] Kim Suhang (1629~1689): Munch'ung is his posthumous title. A late Chosŏn period literary man, he was exiled to Chindo Island in 1689 during the Kisa political upheaval and poisoned to death.

a deep grudge dyed the ground from which dark red flowers opened.
A sacred dragon changed into a fish, mice into tigers.[86]
Their whereabouts are obscure—like things of the past and present.
Traces of them survive in their handwriting in a few papers.
I don't dare look at them, my tears fall like rain.

In the Sinim Massacre of scholars, during King Kyŏngjong's reign, Vice Minister Kim Chekyŏm was exiled to this town, then forced to drink poison and died. His father Ch'angjip, grandfather Suhang, and son Sŏnghaeng[87] were also poisoned for their integrity.

---

[86] Refers to a time when royal subjects took control of national politics, ignoring the king. See Li Bai's poem, "Separating Far Away" (遠別離 Yuanbieli): "When the king loses his subjects, a dragon changes into a fish. When power flows to the king's subjects, mice change into tigers."

[87] Sŏnghaeng (1696-1722): Kim Chekyŏm's eldest son was imprisoned in the Sinim Massacre and tortured nine times, but he denied any wrongdoing until he died. After ascending to the throne, King Yŏngjo wrote a funeral ode to memorialize him.

31. Hong Sŏngmin Who Illuminated Humanity

I ask, what do you think
of our beloved northern seaside?
In the old days, Puryŏng townsmen knew nothing of the humanities
until Hong Chorong[88] came to teach them.
He transcribed an entire set of *The Five Classics*,
sincerely taught the ignorant by day and night.
Two hundred years have passed since the tree fell and flowers withered.
Who knows how much we owe him?
Now only a few of his manuscripts remain,
and many wrong letters were carved into the jujube woodblock.
Good intentions have always suffered the same fate.
Didn't you see people weeping bitterly when the road was blocked?[89]

Lord Munjŏng Hong Sŏngmin was exiled to this town and stayed in Pak Sun's house at Ch'ŏngam. He opened a school to instruct students in the humanities. There are printed woodblock books of Chorongjip *in Puryŏng.*

---

[88] Chorong is the penname of Hong Sŏngmin, a scholar from the middle Chŏsun period. Because of a dispute over the crown prince's installation in 1591, he was exiled to Puryŏng and released in 1592. His posthumous epithet is Lord Munjŏng.

[89] One of the Seven Sages of the Bamboo Grove, 阮籍 Ruan Ji is said to have driven his cart recklessly; when the road was closed, he cried and turned around.

THINKING WINDOW VERSES

32. *Sŭng Kim Invited Me*

I ask, what do you think
of our beloved northern seaside?
Sŭng Kim of Kangch'on sent an ox-cart
to take me to a drinking party, where I spent a merry night.
The house with curved handrails was quiet and cool;
bright lights glittered on the lamppost;
the green wine in the red Chinese jar overflowed;
jade cups and silver bowls were passed around and around.
He hired women to make side dishes for the drinks;
the chicken boiled in soy sauce and the raw trout were excellent.
He eased the pain of my wandering life.
I owe him a lifelong debt of gratitude.

Kangch'on is a placename. Manager Kim's name is Sanggi, and his other name is Yusŏng. His great grandfather, Hasŏng, owned the house in which Chukch'wi Kim Chekyŏm[90] lived. Sanggi took care of the gisaengs in the Pu, who were good, virtuous singers.

---

[90] His penname was Chukch'wi, and he was the son of Prime Minster Kim Ch'angjip. In the massacre of scholars in 1772, the king ordered his father to be poisoned on Kŏjedo Island, and he was exiled to Puryŏng, where he was also poisoned.

KIM RYŎ

33. *Kim Chekyŏm's Funeral*

I ask, what do you think
of our beloved northern seaside?
A hundred-year-old man in Puch'un Fortress[91]
came to Ullu[92] to mourn, then left.
When Yŏnggong[93] Chukch'wi met disaster
only one orphan shed any tears.
Regret was endless as tall mountains and deep seas;
his whole family was scattered in the guilt-by–association system.
There was no one to carry the hearse in a strange land,
but chivalrous Ch'ŏmsa Yang[94] paid for pallbearers.
How can one's life end like this?
Even now, my soul shivers in fear.

Ullu is the penname of Sirang[95] Kim Wŏnhaeng, son of Chukch'wi. He lived in exile with his father. When he died, a man called

---

[91] Another name for Puryŏng.

[92] Kim Wŏnhaeng (1702-1772), a scholar in the late Chosŏn dynasty. His other name was Paekch'un, and his pennames were Miho and Ullu. He was the son of Chekyŏm and grandson of Ch'angjip. When Ch'angjip was put to death by poison, and Chekyŏm and his older brother Sŏnghaeng went into exile, where they were put to death, he gave up his dream of becoming a government official and devoted his life to studying.

[93] 令公: The title of second- and third-ranked governmental officials.

[94] 僉使: The third-ranked official at a military post.

[95] 侍郎: An official Chinese title equal to vice-minister. Kim Wŏnhaeng was the third minister in the Ministry of Public Works.

THINKING WINDOW VERSES

Ch'ŏmsa Yang paid the expense of carrying the coffin, but now no one knows who he was.

34. *Mrs. Sŏng's Wine*

I ask, what do you think
of our beloved northern seaside?
Mrs. Sŏng, who lived south of the stone wall around my
    house,
made a living selling exquisite alcohol.
"My father and grandfather lived in Seoul
but were driven to live here by chance."
She was still beautiful at forty,
with a charming face and a raven-colored chignon.
Taking pity on my poor tormented spirit,
she would hand me a bottle over the wall when she filtered
    wine.
The rice and millet harvests were good last fall,
she must have brewed a thousand jars over the winter.

South of my rented house lived a woman named Sŏng Hwasŏn. Her father was originally from Seoul. Widowed early, she brewed alcohol to sell and was a good friend to Yŏnhŭi.

35. At the Double Ninth Festival[96]

I ask, what do you think
of our beloved northern seaside?
I went to San'gosujangnu[97] Pavilion
to gaze at the sky above my hometown.
Yŏnhŭi's house was nearby, east of the pavilion,
and she was alone, smoothing her silk gauze garment.
When she heard I was at the pavilion, she sent me rice wine,
Hongha wine[98] brimming in an indigo jar.
I drank my fill, and when I raised my head to laugh
only the cloud blocking the sun filled my eyes.
Worldly affairs make no sense anymore.
Getting drunk and living in obscurity may be best.

The last Toho Governor, Yi Yŏjŏl,[99] built his command post on the northeastern corner of the fortress and named it San'gosujang Pavilion, which stands in the mountains, surrounded by cliffs, and commands a fine view.

---

[96] The ninth day of the ninth month on the lunar calendar, the date on which people used to climb a mountain to prevent misfortune.
[97] The literal meaning is a high mountain and a long river pavilion.
[98] The literal meaning is red-mist wine.
[99] A military official in the late Chosŏn period, regarded as an excellent man, who was district magistrate of Puryŏng in 1790 until he was transferred to Ch'angwŏn in 1793.

36. *Pak Sŏngsin, an Excellent Calligrapher*

I ask, what do you think
of our beloved northern seaside?
I liked Pak Sŏngsin, who lived on the east side of town;
his brush strokes were firm, like those of Wijin China.[100]
When he was young, he studied under Wŏnkyo[101]
and wrote on paper thousands of times until it was worn out.
His writing had strong bones, no flesh,
and was comparable to Chuknam[102] and Paekha.[103]
Though small in frame, he was broad-minded
and magnanimous when he had a drinking bowl in his hands.
Sŏngsin, Sŏngsin, my dear friend,
how can I fly free to meet you?

Pak Sŏngsin's name is Kyŏngsil; his penname is Tamsu. He is an army officer. Wŏnkyo is Yi Tobo's penname. Chuknam Oh Chun and Paekha Yun Sun are famous calligraphers.

---

[100] Wei (魏) and Jin (晋) China.
[101] Yi Kwangsa's penname. See #17.
[102] Oh Chun (1587-1666), a civil magistrate and calligrapher in the late Chosŏn period. Chuknam was his penname.
[103] Yun Sun (1680-1741), a civil magistrate and calligrapher in the late Chosŏn period. Yi Kwangsa studied under him.

THINKING WINDOW VERSES

37. *The Duck Hawks Raised by Kiwi Chang*[104]

I ask, what do you think
of our beloved northern seaside?
Kiwi Chang, eight feet tall and fair complexioned,
raised two smart, quick hawks.
The bigger one was black as ink,
and the smaller, braver one was white.
His yellow eyes and white talons never missed his prey,
all day he stared at the floating clouds.
When I asked Chang for the white one, he gave me the black one,
which saddened me for a long while.
Now all, alas, has come to nothing.
I finally realize my desire is futile.

Kiwi's name was Ilhwan, his other name was Musuk. He was Hŭiwik's maternal uncle.

---

[104] 騎衛: A low-ranking military official in the cavalry.

38. Sŏ Myŏngwŏn's Cat

I ask, what do you think
of our beloved northern seaside?
The cat in old Mr. Sŏ's house was charming as crystal
and had a knack for catching mice.
It had a brown nose, woke up early in the morning,
hunted around mouse holes, bit and shook mice.
Its front paws danced while its hind paws stayed low;
it pretended to move forward but jumped instead.
The mouse, emerging, cowering, stayed still.
The cat pounced and snatched it up, as if cupping a dove.
Why do officials at the national treasury[105] worry about the grain mice steal?
Why not bet big money on this cat?

Old Mr. Sŏ is Sŏ Myŏngwŏn.[106]

---

[105] The government office responsible for issuing salaries to civil servants.
[106] The owner of the house Kim Ryŏ rented in Puryŏng.

39. *Kungyang Papers from Ch'okye*

I ask, what do you think
of our beloved northern seaside?
A box of Kungyang papers[107] from Ch'okye[108]
was sent to me from Yunin's son.
Light blue, lemon yellow, purple, yellow, and red papers,
with delicate, uniform patterns, shining brightly.
They were strong, soft, oily smooth;
the bamboo papers from Honam Province[109] proved to be inferior.
Having loved Yunin, I cherished these papers, wrapping them in many layers,
giving none away, not even when Konso[110] pleaded with me.
Like a storm-tossed boat, my body wanders here and there.
I ask you not to feel bitter because of the paper.

Yunin was Sirang Kim Chosun,[111] and his other name was Much'ŏm. The bamboo paper made in Honam Province was regarded as the best.

---

[107] Papers used in the Royal Palace.
[108] A town in Ch'okye-myŏn, Hapch'ŏn-gun in Kyŏngnam Province, which produced high-quality rice paper.
[109] Thin paper made of young bamboo, also called bamboo leaf paper.
[110] Nam Hŭngyu: an associate of Kim Ryŏ in Puryŏng, regarded as a good poet.
[111] Kim Chosun (1765-1832): A late Chosŏn period civil official, the fourth generation of Kim Ch'angjip; Yunin was his penname. A close friend of Kim Ryŏ, they edited Uch'osokchi together. He secured Kim's release from exile in Chinhae as well as civil official positions.

KIM RYŎ

40. *An Inkstone from Hŭksimha*

I ask, what do you think
of our beloved northern seaside?
The shape of this antique Hŭksimha inkstone is eccentric.
I bought it from a merchant in Sŏnsŏng village.
On its dark red base are stacked dotted yellow layers,
ripples surge on the rolling green stripes,
and bamboo is engraved on the rims of the bowl
within which water is stored and flows,
raising purple clouds. Delicately trimmed and carved,
this must be the work of a master craftsman.
Overnight I was exiled to the south.
Alas, you have become like a discarded strainer.

Hŭksimha is south of Yŏnggo. Sŏnsŏng is a village in Yŏnggo.

41. *Poor Old Man Chang*

I ask, what do you think
of our beloved northern seaside?
Old man Chang had literary talent—and no luck.
His grey hair was busy during the season of the state examination.
He was fluent in *Four Books* and *Three Classics;*[112]
three times he passed the local tests only to fail the national exams.
His prolific writings, tucked away in boxes,
are still the talk of young people in the town.
I also took the national exams many times.
Weighed against him, I should retire to samsa.[113]
And yet he is a ruined man, discarded in a sandstorm.
Few recognized his remarkable talent.

The elder Chang's name is Chaejong, and his other name is Chaang. He is Paengnŭng's father. He took and failed the national exams many times.

---

[112] The authoritative books of Confucianism, the first four being *Great Learning, The Doctrine of the Mean, Analects,* and *Mencius,* and then the three classics, *The Book of Odes, The Books of Documents,* and the *I Ching.*
[113] Samsa is ninety li away (about thirty-six kms), a three-day's walk for the army.

42. Changŭi[114] Kim, a Sophist

I ask, what do you think
of our beloved northern seaside?
I didn't know that Changŭi Kim of Ch'ŏngjin loved
   debating so much.
He wore nice clothes with a loose belt and carried a
   goosefoot cane.
His hair was grey, his beard reached to his belly,
and his sophist arguments about a frog with a tail
or a three-legged chicken rivaled those of Tamch'ŏn-
   gaeg.[115]
When he visited me last winter, he had
a heated discussion with Old Ch'a about righteousness.
When I took Ch'a's side,
everyone clapped their hands in delight.

Ch'ŏngjin is another name for Ch'ŏngam. Channgŭi Kim's name is Ch'angjŏng, and his other name is Iyŏp. He is Sanggi's uncle and an eloquent speaker. Elder Ch'a is Namgyu.

---

[114] 掌議: Student representative at Sŏngkyunkwan and a county school.
[115] 談天客: Refers to 鄒衍, Zou Yan, a Qi dynasty philosopher from the Yin and Yang School, who was learned in almost every branch of science. His name has become synonymous with eloquence.

THINKING WINDOW VERSES

43. *Young Sŏk*

I ask, what do you think
of our beloved northern seaside?
Young Sŏk lived in front of Hyŏngjeam;
his unruly hair covered his shoulders.
He was reading books by the age of eight or nine,
kneeling and making a deep bow to his elders.
He was short but swift-footed—
townspeople called him "a flying squirrel."
He visited my rented room to study *The Book of Filial Duty*,
lodging every lesson deep in his heart.
He would knock on my door after running through the
    endless rain,
barefoot in the long summer rainy season.

Hyŏngjeam is the name of a mountain. Ijang was the young boy's name; his other name was Hwanji. His brother's name was Ihwan and his other name was Changji. He was a scholar.

44. *Sheepskin Cloth*

I ask, what do you think
of our beloved northern seaside?
I received a green silk oja[116] lined with sheepskin.
Yŏnhŭi made it with her own hands.
It was one cha[117] and six ch'i[118] long, wide half of its length.
The front was not sewn together but opened in the middle.
Four-sevenths of the circumference of each armpit was sewn,
composed of three hems, two open in front and one in back.
The left sleeve was long, the right was half its length,
the cloth string round-knotted with aligning ties.
Now even a cha of fabric is hard to find
to hide my elbow in a ragged summer jacket.

On seeing this phrase in the Analects, *"For everyday fur clothes, he made the lower ends long and the right sleeve short," Yŏnhŭi made a sheepskin oja with a short sleeve. You can find more details in* The Chronicle of Yŏnhŭi's Sayings and Doings.

---

[116] A lined jacket shorter than a long coat and longer than a *chŏgori*, the upper garment in traditional Korean clothing.
[117] Traditional measure of length, about 30.3 cm.
[118] Traditional measure of length, one-tenth of a cha, 3.03 cm.

THINKING WINDOW VERSES

45. *Namp'yŏng Fan*

I ask, what do you think
of our beloved northern seaside?
A new Namp'yông fan for Dano Day,
its bamboo ribs spreading from the fish head inlaid with
    ivory.
Yakwŏnkŏsa Kim Sôkch'i[119] painted
on it an extraordinary landscape then wrote,
"Green river and white rock, a road for fishermen
and woodsmen, many valleys and peaks at twilight."
I kept it in a bamboo box
to preserve it from dust and damage—in vain.
But what use is there to think of it in this seaside of agony,
where hot winds blow and poisonous fumes rise?

Namp'yŏng is a town in Honam Province, which produced high-quality fans. Sŏkch'i is my friend Kim Cho Myŏngwŏn.[120] *His other name is Myŏngwŏn, and he is a fine painter. The quoted phrase is the title of his painting.*

---

[119] Kim Cho (1754-1825): His penname was Sŏkhan or Sŏkch'I, and his other name was Myŏngwŏn—a literary man and artist living in the country, without a civil service appointment.

[120] Here Cho was his name and Myŏngwŏn was his other name. It was a custom to use one's family name first, then his name, and then his other name.

46. *Hearing of My Father's Death*

I ask, what do you think
of our beloved northern seaside?
Even the snowy wind wailed in Hansik[121] that February.
How to describe my mourning to the end of the sky?[122]
After pleading in vain to heaven and earth,
I shed tears stamping my feet, looking southward.
Everyone has parents, and parents have children,
but how have I alone become a confined man.
In the three years since my father's death I haven't visited
    his grave.
I'm filled with regret, bleeding from my nine holes.[123]
The ford and ridge of Tugok is two thousand li away.
Who will pay their respects at the grave, comfort my
    father's soul?

My father died on January 19, 1799, in the 23rd year of Chŏngjo's reign. But I didn't hear the news until February 29th. My parents' graves are in Tugok, Kongju.

---

[121] A traditional holiday in Korea, the 195th day after the winter solstice. People usually visit their ancestors' graves to pay their respects and cut the grass.
[122] Mourning to the end of the sky means to cry until one's body fails. Refers to the death of one's parents.
[123] The nine orifices of the human body.

47. *Mr. Yi, the Filial Son of Puryŏng*

I ask, what do you think
of our beloved northern seaside?
Mr. Yi is generally regarded as the most filial son in Puryŏng.
He lost his parents early and had no one to rely on.
Five brothers lived together,
their brotherly love stronger than Kanggoeng of the Han dynasty.[124]
When one of his brothers got sick and died, he lamented bitterly,
vomited blood, beat his breast.
After he dressed the corpse, he took to his sickbed;
he had sores in his eyes, his face turned black.
Four-foot twin graves next to the road—
passers-by look at them and cry.

The name of the filial son is Yi Sangsŏng; his other name is Kunsuk. He was a petty official in the town. His four brothers are Sangbin, Sangch'un, Sangŏk, and Sangwi. I wrote The Remaining Stories of the Filial Son Yi *separately.*

---

[124] 姜肱 Jianggong, renowned in the Han dynasty for his love of his two younger brothers.

48. *The Demise of King Chŏngjo*[125]

I ask, what do you think
of our beloved northern seaside?
There was a big earthquake in June,
crows and magpies died, bushes and grass caught fire.[126]
Unlucky living souls lost their majesty,
government officials rushed to the palace gate in bare feet.
Unable to express his humble respects,
a lonely vassal[127] wiped his bloody tears away and stifled his cry in vain.
The moment that evil news arrived is still vivid to me:
the sun was dull in the dark sky, there was an angry gust of wind.
Farmers put down their plows, women rushed here and there.
The mountains and fields cried, shaking like water boiling in a kettle.

King Chŏngjo died on June 28, 1800, though the news did not arrive until July 8.

---

[125] The 22nd king of the Chosŏn dynasty reigned from 1776-1800, inaugurating the Restoration of Literary Style, a movement to restore the pure classical style of writing in the face of the current popular style. He denigrated Kim Ryŏ, who wrote novels in this new style.
[126] All these phenomena are not literal but metaphorical.
[127] Refers to Kim Ryŏ himself.

49. *Sagan*[128] *Oh T'aeŏn*[129]

I ask, what do you think
of our beloved northern seaside?
How poor you are, Sagan Oh of Suju!
We met when you rode to see me last fall.
We sat face to face, joyfully, through the long night.
You were as anxious about current affairs as for your old friend.
When you pointed at Ch'ang'o,[130] we both sobbed.
You came here to console me and burned your face while we played.
Time passes like a running colt seen through a hole in the door.
In a flash we part in life, and separate forever when we die.
After your funeral procession somberly headed north,
I could not even turn my head toward the land of Yuryŏng

Suju is another name for Hoeryŏng. Sagan's name is T'aeôn, and his other name is Hŭibo. Running to pay his respects to the Royal Portrait in Insan, where Chŏngjo's royal tomb is located, he dropped dead in the street. Yuryŏng is a mountain pass in Hoeryŏng.

---

[128] 司諫 The third-ranked official in the Censors Office, in charge of expostulating to the king.
[129] He was born in 1732 and passed the Special Examination in Hamgyŏng Province in 1774.
[130] 蒼梧 Cangwu: Another name for Jiuyishsn (九疑山), where Emperor Shun is buried in the royal mausoleum.

50. *The West Pavilion of Puryŏng*

I ask, what do you think
of our beloved northern seaside?
The western gate pavilion of Puryŏng Fortress is one
　　hundred ch'ŏk high;
when you look downstream, it's dark green.
A hundred houses for civilians are located by the stream,
their Korean spindle tree fences and cedar gates reflecting
　　in the water.
The early morning smoke from breakfast preparations in
　　the village
hangs in the boughs and shines bright as twilight.
Once I climbed up to the pavilion
and wandered leisurely, enjoying the landscape.
My heart still wanders on the east side
of the stepping stone bridge where horses roam.

THINKING WINDOW VERSES

51. *Fishing in the River*

I ask, what do you think
of our beloved northern seaside?
When apricot flowers fall and millet buds sprout,
trout swim toward the bend in the river.
On a day of drizzle around the Chajangdam Pond
the water was deep, rocks were few, and the fish were fat.
Village men came with fishing spears
and scraped moss from the rocks.
The fisheyes we boiled in an earthenware brazier were fresh,
the makgeolli in the bowls and jars had a beautiful color.
I ask my fishing friends from the eastern house,
"Are you talking about this man in the south this year?"

The Chajangdam pond, located forty li from the village, had odd rocks and plenty of trout.

52. *At the Last Dano Festival*

I ask, what do you think
of our beloved northern seaside?
Last Dano, just after the rain stopped
in the silky fragrant grasses and trees by the clear water,
Yŏnhŭi prepared a mal of wine to console me,
lest my heart grow uneasy.
She served not only raw Anjin trout
but also ball cakes made of Murŭng oats.
This Dano brings more agony;
vipers are everywhere in the sizzling heat of the miasmal
   sea.
I am too sick and weak to stand.
I enter the bamboo forest and lay my head down on a stone
   pillow.

Anjin, where trout are caught, is in Yŏnchŏn. Murŭng is another name for Musan.

THINKING WINDOW VERSES

53. *At Ch'a Tongsuk's House*

I ask, what do you think
of our beloved northern seaside?
I was invited to the house of Ch'a Tongsuk[131]
when the moon rose like a ship in the early autumn night.
Fragrant wine filled cups decorated with partridge spots,
boiled pork shoulder and scarlet marinated crab were served.
Beautiful women paraded before the oil lamp,
T'anang of old,[132] with her charming dimples, was there.
Your song and my dance had yet to finish,
but it was bright in the east and the starlight was already white.
When we reluctantly parted in front of the fortress,
the cry of cranes sounded on the slope of the green mountain.

On a moonlit early autumn night in Pu[133] *gisaeng Yang Kwanok and I had a drinking party in the house of Ach'o Ch'a. I played geomungo*[134] *and Kwanok sang songs.*

---

[131] The other name of the guard Cha Ijin. See #11.
[132] 妥娘 Tuo Niang: a female singer from Jinling (Nanjing's former name), China. 王士禎 Wang Shizhen refers to Tuo Niang and Shi Niang, Ming dynasty gisaengs, at "脫十娘鄭妥娘 Teng Shi Niang Zheng Tou Niang" in his novel, 池北偶談 *Chibe Evening Talk*.
[133] Pu is an administrative area in the To, equivalent to a province or state.
[134] A six-stringed Korean zither.

54. Chi Tŏkhae, Who Read Books Even on Military Strategy

I ask, what do you think
of our beloved northern seaside?
All the young men in this northern area were robust,
but twenty-year-old Chi Tŏkhae was the best.
He was seven chŏk tall, with handsome eyebrows;
the spot in the middle of his forehead shone like amethyst.
With a slender waist and stout build, he was a fine marksman from a horse,
and knew five books on military science thoroughly.
From diligent study of history he was learned in things past and present.
In discussions about success and failure, he never failed.
Heaven gave birth to a man to use somewhere,
but why is he wasting his time in this backwater?

Tŏkhae's other name was Kyeham. He was a military officer attached to the headquarters. He was Yŏnhŭi's third cousin. The military book referred to is Pyŏnghakchinam.[135]

---

[135] 兵學之南: An edited version of 戚繼光 Qi Jiguang's 紀效新書 *Jixiaoxinshu*. Qi Jiguang was a Ming dynasty general who fought in the Japanese invasion of Korea. The book appeared in 1787.

THINKING WINDOW VERSES

55. *Crystal-like Kim Sŏngwŏn*

I ask, what do you think
of our beloved northern seaside?
Young Kim Sŏngwŏn was extraordinarily talented,
clear as ice in all things, shining like crystal.
His spirit was close to Tao, he resembled Yŏmong.[136]
He would recite the nine thoughts[137] and follow the nine behaviors.[138]
He could write large letters, and his brush strokes were straight.
Courteous from childhood, he folded his hands, took short polite steps.

---

[136] 冉雍 Ranyong: A Confucianism scholar in the Lu dynasty; his other name was Zhonggong, and he excelled in virtuous deeds, stressing the importance of studying ritual.

[137] The nine thoughts a nobleman should always keep in mind, from *The Analects of Confucius*, Book 16. In observation, he focuses on clarity; in listening, on acuity; in facial expression, on gentleness; in bearing, on reverence; in words, on loyalty; in affairs, on attentiveness; in doubt, on questioning; in anger, on troubling consequences; in opportunities for gain, on what is right.

[138] The nine behaviors a nobleman should follow. "The carriage of a man of rank was easy, but somewhat slow;—grave and reserved, when he saw any one whom he wished to honor. He did not move his feet lightly, nor his hands irreverently. His eyes looked straightforward, and his mouth was kept quiet and composed. No sound from him broke the stillness, and his head was carried upright. His breath came without panting or stoppage, and his standing gave (the beholder) an impression of virtue. His looks were grave, and he sat like an impersonator of the dead." James Legge trans. The Li Ki. Kessinger Publishing, LLC. 2010, 239.

Knowing that life depends upon the lessons of a noble teacher,
he neglected nothing in his fidelity to king, teacher, and parents.
What use are light fur clothes and fat horses
to the children of glamorous high officials?

Kim Sŏngwŏn's name is Chongguk. This son of Pak Kyŏngsil's sister studied under Kim T'aeyo, whose other name is Kyŏnghoe. He was Wŏnkyo's student and learned in rituals.

56. *Gentle Sir Kyŏnghoe*

I ask, what do you think
of our beloved northern seaside?
Who knows rituals among the Confucian scholars in
   Puryŏng?
Sir Kyônghoe is truly gentle and modest,
warm-hearted, frank, natural,
though he is quite strict in his judgments concerning right
   behavior.
Namkyŏ's influence reached Wŏnkyo,
where its ripples finally washed over him.
Once, when Mr. Yi and Mr. Chang had an argument,
he unflinchingly defended the right way.
Meat-eaters[139] are contemptible, like dogs and pigs.
How can we persuade him to edify the world?

Namkyŏ is Lord Munsung Pak Sech'ae.[140] He was Wŏnkyo's teacher. When the townsman Yi Chesŏng did not wear mourning dress after his stepmother died, Chang Chŏngse attacked him, precipitating a lawsuit.

---

[139] A derogatory term for civil officials.
[140] Pak Sech'ae (1631-1695): His penname was Namgye, and his posthumous title was Lord Munsung. He was the second state councilor and learned in the study of rituals.

57. Hwang Taesŏk, a Dead Shot

I ask, what do you think
of our beloved northern seaside?
Hwang Taesŏk was an excellent rider
and archer who never missed his mark.
He had a fine appearance, with thick sideburns,
a slim waist, and monkey-like arms,[141] and he was strong as a bear.
Last spring, in the martial arts competition between Kyŏngsŏng and Puryŏng,
he recorded twenty points in three rounds. What a marvelous feat!
But those damned corrupt officials
refused to award him the prize, ridiculing him instead.
He moaned for a while, then returned home
to plow the edge of the green mountain until the sun went down.

Hwang Taesŏk's other name was Yosin. Hong Kwang'il, Assistant Prefect of Kyŏngsŏng, and Yu Sangnyang,[142] Regional Military Commander, held a martial arts competition between the two towns. Hwang Taesŏk placed first, but Yu did not award him the prize.

---

[141] The phrase means his arms were so long they dropped below his knees, and he had the force of a military man. The expression was also used to describe a good bowman.

[142] Yu Sangnyang (1764- ?): A military official in the late Chosŏn period. His other name was Kyŏngnyong. After passing the military examination, he was Military Commander of Puryŏng, Army Commander of Kyŏngsangu-do Province, Army Commander of P'yŏngan Province, and Commander of the Capital Garrison.

THINKING WINDOW VERSES

58. *My Brother Sŏwŏn's Scrapbooks*

I ask, what do you think
of our beloved northern seaside?
Sŏwŏn[143] sent me some drafts of texts,
which I kept in a dusty case, like gold nuggets.
P'albun[144] came back wrapped in Hŭiik's[145] cloth.
Haengch'o[146] suffered Kyeham's[147] ridicule again.
A rare gift of his writings arrived,
with Kapsan weasel hair[148] stiffer than steel.
When the military camp officer made a row this spring,
I lost these things in the ensuing panic.
I did not follow your advice to be prudent,
and click my tongue, and sigh in grief. Only grasshoppers
    chirp in vain.

I had Sŏwŏn's eight-fold P'albun and an eight-fold Haengch'o.

---

[143] Kim Ryŏ's brother, Kim Sŏn's penname. Accused of involvement with Kang Ich'ŏn's so-called "Vulgar Words Criminal Cases," he was exiled to Ch'osan near the Yalu River in 1801. He passed the civil examination in 1820 and worked as Royal Secretary-transmitter. Kim Ryŏ rated him one of the four best poets of his time, along with Yi Usin, Yi Chero, and Kim Sŏnsin.
[144] A style of calligraphy invented by Cai Yong in the Han dynasty, twenty percent of which is composed in the ornamental style, the rest in the seal character style.
[145] The other name of Kim Hyŏngyu, Kim Ryŏ's student.
[146] Semi-cursive and cursive styles of calligraphy.
[147] The other name of Chi Tŏkhae, Yŏnhŭi's third cousin.
[148] Kapsan is a northeastern county in South Hamgyŏng Province, where stiff slender brushes are made with weasel hair.

KIM RYŎ

Knowing that the State Tribunal Officer was coming, Yi Pyŏngjŏng sent a military officer to seize my writings and drafts of texts.

59. *Yŏnhŭi's Aunt*

I ask, what do you think
of our beloved northern seaside?
A silk pocket with a purple string, embroidered
with Chinese ink-colored grapes and images of the sun and
   moon.
Yŏnhŭi's aunt lives in Yuju,
and her husband travels to Yŏnggot'ap in Manchuria to sell
   goods.
Someone delivered a sealed letter in the pocket,
its color hasn't faded even after three years in the box.
Life is so difficult and sad because the news carried
by geese flying south and carp swimming north was cut
   off.[149]
Fleas and lice are busy on my short, tattered kudzu cloth.
We only miss each other forever until this life ends.

Yuju is a place in Hoeryŏng. The surname of Yŏnhŭi's maternal cousin is Kal.

---

[149] Geese and carp are traditional carriers of letters.

60. *My Late Father's Dog-eared Book,* Collected Commentaries on the Shang Shu

I ask, what do you think
of our beloved northern seaside?
Sir Kubong wrote *Collected Commentaries on the Shang Shu,*[150]
which my father copied out and read a thousand times.
The red circles and blue dots[151] he marked in the book are still vivid,
a mellow fragrance still lingers there.
He even drew Yugong's map[152] by himself;
the mountains and rivers are so vivid you can almost touch them.
He suffered years of mountains collapsing and seas dividing
but never failed to adjust his attire, though his *Six Classics*[153] burned to ash.
Thanks to his poor son, he can never close his eyes
even in death, saddled with a thousand-year-long grudge.

---

[150] Sir Kubong is Cai Shen, a Confucian scholar of the Southern Song. *Collected Commentaries on the Shang Shu* (尚書傳) is his commentary on *Ancient Documents*.
[151] The circle and dot drawn in a book to mark important passages.
[152] 禹貢圖: Yugong divided China into nine districts; the map is thus Yugong's nine-district map.
[153] Refers to *The Book of Changes, The Book of Documents, The Book of Odes, The Book of Rituals, Spiring and Autumn Annals,* and *The Book of Music*.

THINKING WINDOW VERSES

61. *Yŏnhŭi Plays "Paektuŭm"*[154]

I ask, what do you think
of our beloved northern seaside?
On a moon-bright night in Paekchung[155] last year
we took our leisure in her pavilion.
I hugged her, and she picked up her geomungo
to play Munkun's "Paektuŭm."
But then she put it down and wept,
saying "Playing this tune, I hear the sound of separation."
Her words have stayed in my ear ever since.
How could she foretell the turmoil rising from the flatlands?
A white crane flies east, a swallow, west,
and in between the three-thousand-li Yaksu[156] divides us.

---

[154] 白頭吟 Baitouyin: 文君 Zhuo Wenjun was a female writer in the Han dynasty. When her husband Sima Xiangru tried to take a woman from Maoling as a concubine, she wrote a poem to announce the end of their relationship. He changed his mind: "I hoped to get a same-minded person and not to be separated until our hair turns grey." But there is some controversy about its authorship.

[155] July 15th on the lunar calendar, which is All Souls Day in Buddhism.

[156] 弱水 Ruo Shui: A major river system in northern China, which flows approximately 630 kilometers from its headwaters on the northern Gansu side of the Qilian Mountains. It is said that even goose feathers sink in river water.

KIM RYŎ

62. Summer in Okp'oktong

I ask, what do you think
of our beloved northern seaside?
A thousand kil-high waterfall forms a stream in the
    Okp'oktong valley,
and a Korean spindle tree stands on a broad flat rock.
A clear wind blows over the tree, and the stream meanders,
and you don't know whether the muggy summer heat is
    real or not.
After loitering on the trail, I lie down under the spindle tree,
where the falling petals make a cushion.
Poor me! This year the sea is hot, coated with a damp,
    poisonous air,
and swarms of black flies and red scorpions bite me.
The little bamboo and bushy bamboo provide no shelter.
Who can endure under this blazing red sun?

The Okp'oktong cave is located ten li north of town.

63. Chu Hoegoe's [157] Edited Version of Central Harmony

I ask, what do you think
of our beloved northern seaside?
Stamped in *Central Harmony*, edited by Chu Hoegoe,
is a small seal of Min Chijae.
I borrowed it from Wŏlli; every character
was correctly arranged on the ginkgo block bordered with silk.
I kept it with utmost care
lest it be ruined, gnawed at by a mouse.
The vicissitudes of life are so severe
I'm reduced to eating broiled bat meat this spring.
If I can't keep my friend's book until the end,
isn't my life a source of shame to the memory of Kangnok?[158]

Chu Hoego's name is *Shixian* (士顯). The renowned scholar Min Chijae's name was Chinhu; his other name was Chŏngnŭng. He served the nation as a minister; his posthumous title is Ch'ungmun. Min Wŏlli's name is Ch'ibok, and he is Chije's great-great-grandson.

---

[157] 周會魁 Zhou Huikui: 周士顯 Zhou Shixian's penname. He corrected *Four Books* 四書大全, which were published in eighteen volumes. *Central Harmony* is in two volumes.

[158] 江祿 Jiang Lu: A Liang dynasty scholar famous for his careful handling of books.

64. *Landscape after Heavy Rain*

I ask, what do you think
of our beloved northern seaside?
Heavy rain fell for ten days, as if the sky had been punctured,
and deep water poured over the plain to form a sea.
The water in the valley increased, the river overflowed.
The Masang ship[159] reached the empty valley east of the bridge.
Only branches rose above the water, rice and millet sank underwater,
frogs and narrow-mouthed toads spawned in the kitchen;
mudfish swam in the kettle.
Oarsmen netted salmon with mottled nets
and sold them in the stall in front of Yŏnhŭi's house.
She stood against the handrail,
shrieking in delight, as we watched how the water flowed.

There was an empty valley five li south of the town. At the entrance was a bridge fifty li from the sea. Last summer, in heavy rain, a ship sailed past the bridge and anchored under the fortress.

---

[159] A ship used to carry soldiers, grain, and supplies in P'yŏngan and Hamgyŏng Provinces.

THINKING WINDOW VERSES

65. *Japanese Sword*

I ask, what do you think
of our beloved northern seaside?
A Tanju sword,[160] whose handle and sheath
are made of eaglewood,[161] shone like a mirror.
I polished it with dabchick oil[162] from Chŏnho,
and affixed to it a fine butterfly string from Kisŏng.
The sharp blade and back of the sword were engraved with
    a dragon pattern;
one touch of the blade would split a hair.
I caressed and cared for it, as if it were my young mistress.
Even Makya and Kanjang[163] were no better than you.
When the autumn rains fell and the wind blew,
the sword cried by itself on an old wall in the back of the
    house.

Tanju is another name for Japan. There is a place called Chŏnpo in Paech'ŏn-gun, Hwanghae Province. Dabchicks are produced there. Kisŏng is Pyŏngyang.

---

[160] Japanese sword.
[161] Fragrant wood that comes from India and Southeast Asia.
[162] Dabchick oil is used to clean and rust-proof swords.
[163] Both 鎮鋣 Moye and 干將 Ganjiang are legendary swords made by Moye and Ganjang, blacksmiths from Wu China.

66. *Pine Mushrooms*

I ask, what do you think
of our beloved northern seaside?
When the frost-tipped boughs are dense as snow,
and green leaves turn red, and geese cry sadly,
pine mushrooms sprout everywhere, though the best
are on the slope called Yŏnji Hill on Ch'ŏnggye Mountain.
Young mushrooms with clenched hands and old ones with
    open caps
abound, as if cultivated in the moldy earth.
People climb there to pick them, carrying baskets and
    hampers.[164]
They boil water to blanch them and rinse them in clear
    water.
The mushrooms are fragrant, the soft ones used for soup,
    the hard ones broiled.
They should be included in a sumptuous feast.

Ch'ŏnggye Mountain is located thirty li east of Pu. It has a long slope called Yŏnji Hill, because Yŏnji pear trees grow beside it.

---

[164] A box-shaped wicker basket.

67. *The Magpies of Puryŏng*

I ask, what do you think
of our beloved northern seaside?
A magpie raised two chicks in its nest, in the cedar tree in
  the yard,
until a rat snake bit it, orphaning them.
I hated the snake so much I stabbed it with a stick,
saving the two chicks, which I carefully raised.
They grew up to catch and eat worms,
to go out in the morning and return to the eaves at sunset.
Early one morning I heard a sad croak.
That was the day an official from the state tribunal came to
  arrest me.[165]
Magpies are just animals, but they know nature's secrets,
crying bitterly with long and short notes.

---

[165] Refers to the arrival of an official from the State Tribunal to transfer Kim Ryŏ to Seoul.

68. *My Winter in Pat'aŏm*

I ask, what do you think
of our beloved northern seaside?
A thousand chŏk of snow in front of Pat'aŏm,[166]
and thick red clouds in the night sky, and a bleak wind
    howling.
Snow flowers and sleet fell on the clear stream,
the wrinkled river was frozen hard as glass.
Icicles hung from an exile's beard,
my ten fingers were so numb I couldn't spread them.
With a water bottle on my back, I went through the gate
and walked on the snow-covered ice to the cold waterside.
By now the wine must be ripe at Yi Asŏm's house,
where the blue lamplight shone bright south of the Sŏggyo
    Bridge.

There was a rock cave in the back yard of Myŏngwŏn, which I called Pat'a Cave the year I lived there. Asŏm was a local gisaeng.

---

[166] 波吒广: Pat'a Cave. Pat'a means hardship.

69. *Corn*

I ask, what do you think
of our beloved northern seaside?
People in Pukkwan[167] grow corn like greens,
planting more than ten furrows to a field.
In the summer, corn cobs grow larger than cucumbers
and silky silver corn tassels flutter.
Their round kernels are as big as pomegranates,
yellow, purple, black, and white.
Steamed in a kettle, they're delicious
and fill you up, they're good for your stomach.
Customs vary in different regions;
corn is despised in the south but valued in Pukkwan.

---

[167] Another name for Hamgyŏng Province.

70. *Pijang*[168] *Yi of Sŏjin*

I ask, what do you think
of our beloved northern seaside?
What a nice person Pijang Yi of Sŏjin is!
He must have been Chuga[169] or Wŏnang[170] in a previous life.
He didn't need a thousand pieces of gold or a high salary,
he provided water for the fish gasping in the cart rut.
How rare it is to be helped when you are in need.
You must engrave his grace into your bones so as not to forget.
The world values a thousand sheepskin coats but hates the coat made from the armpit of a fox.[171]
People say a boar should be castrated;[172] he was stung by bees and scorpions.
The rotating blue sky will surely know

---

[168] A clerk who works for the provincial governor or military commander.
[169] 朱家 Zhujia: A chivalrous Lu dynasty figure, renowned for risking his life to help those in need.
[170] 袁盎 Yuanang: A civil servant in the Qian Han dynasty, known for speaking out directly.
[171] Flattering common people is appreciated more than the words of an upright person. The phrase comes from the Sima Qian's *Records of the Grand Historian*: "The skins of a thousand sheep are better than the hair in the armpit of a fox, and the truthful words of one scholar are better than the flattery of a thousand subjects."
[172] A phrase from the *I-Ching*: "A boar's molar should be removed to make it powerless." Which means the violent and cunning should be removed in advance.

he encountered Tosin[173] like an Asian wild dog and was punished.[174]

Sŏjin is on the border of Kyŏngsŏng. The name of the military clerk is Chungbae; his other name is Taesuk. He was a close friend of mine. He worked for my cousin An[175] until he was arrested and tortured almost to death by Yi Pyŏngjŏng.

---

[173] Another name for a provincial governor.
[174] Refers to Yi Pyŏngjŏng, Governor of Hamgyŏng Province.
[175] Ch'aek, the military commander of Hamgyŏng Province, was Kim Ryŏ's first cousin.

71. *A Young Boy, Ch'a Yaksu*

I ask, what do you think
of our beloved northern seaside?
Ch'a Yaksu was an intelligent boy
whose ancestors came from a respectable noble family,
who were condemned to being hacked into pieces and scattered.
Now his family has been forgotten.
He was tall and charming, a fine archer and promising scholar;
his pretty face and black hair were clean and affectionate.
When I greeted him, happily opening the door,
he was wet with dew from the rank grass in the path.
In hard times people cannot help but think of a talented man.
Your elegant presence is vivid in my eyes.

Ch'a Yaksu's name was Sŏngnyu, and he was the son of Yi Kam, Ch'a Ijin's younger brother. I taught him Records of the Grand Historian.[176]

---

[176] 史記 Shiji: A 130-volume history compiled by 司馬遷 Sima Qian of the Han dynasty, recording Chinese history from the Yellow Emperor to Emperor Wu of the Han dynasty.

THINKING WINDOW VERSES

72. *Kulloes[177] of Puryŏng*

I ask, what do you think
of our beloved northern seaside?
Kulloes of Puryŏng running amok,
you must be angels of death disguised as humans.
Like wildcats, the three Yi brothers
enjoyed killing and burying people to leave no traces.
To capture the regional military commander,
they plotted to burn down the royal plate.[178]
Besides them, Tŭkhyŏn and Tŏkp'il
were also wicked, cunning, and treacherous.
When Sir Hwangjangmok[179] started his new post,
these rascals ran wild, as if the world belonged to them.

I wrote about the affair of the three Yi brothers of Pongsŏk, Pongsam, and Ponghwa, and Kim Tŭkhyŏn and Kim Tŏkp'il and the regional military commander, Yi Yŏjŏl, in Yŏnŭm *Essay. Sir Hwangjangmok is Yu Sangnyang.*

---

[177] Kulloe is a military policeman in charge of prisoners in the Government Office.

[178] A wooden plate on which the character Chŏn (殿) (Royal Palace) was engraved: a symbol for the king. Twice each month, on the first and fifteenth, all government workers gathered and bowed twice before the plate. Damaging or insulting it was regarded as lese-majesty. The criminal and head officer were punished for such infractions.

[179] Hwangjangmok is the high-quality pine used for coffins. Sir Hwangjangmok refers to Yu Sangnyang, because he embezzled pine trees that should have gone to the king's office.

73. Mr. Ch'oe, a Village School Teacher

I ask, what do you think
of our beloved northern seaside?
What a kind person was Ch'oe,
who taught for more than forty years?
Knowing only a few characters, unable to distinguish 魚
    from 魯,
how could he teach classics and history?
His distortions were ridiculous,
everything was confusing; nothing was clear.
He had many students,
none of them any good at anything.
He was such an ignorant quack.
My face still burns whenever I hear about him.

Ch'oe Yangjung from Chŏnju was exiled to this place and opened a school from which none of his many students amounted to anything.

74. Governor Yi Pyŏngjŏng

I ask, what do you think
of our beloved northern seaside?
Ch'umil Ku,[180] Special Army Envoy last year,
none can compete with him in righteousness and cleanliness.
The new governor, Sangsŏ Yi,[181]
is vile and envious and loves extortion.
Unsatisfied with exacting outrageous taxes,
he brought complete ruin to the areas north of Ch'ŏllyŏnggwan.[182]
He gives a prize to cruel workers and fires upright ones.
People cower, preparing to leave.
Rain won't fall until Sang Hongyang[183] is boiled to death.
Farmers and women weep by the brook.

When Lord Ku Ik[184] came as Special Army Envoy, people loved his righteousness. But when his successor, Yi Pyŏngjŏng, began to exploit and abuse them, rain stopped falling for a long time, making life hard for them. Ch'ŏllyŏnggwan is in Hoeyang.

---

[180] Administer of the Central Council.
[181] Minister, the third-ranked civil official.
[182] The gateway to Ch'ŏllyŏnggwan Pass in Hoeyang, beyond which lies Hamgyŏng Province.
[183] 桑弘羊 Sang Hongyang: A government officer who managed agriculture and the economy in the Han dynasty, levying cruel taxes: a stand-in for Yi Pyŏngjŏng in the poem.
[184] Ku Ik (1737-1804): A civil official in the late Chosŏn period. He was Inspector-General and Governor of Hamgyŏng Province.

75. Mrs. Yuk Cries Bitterly

I ask, what do you think
of our beloved northern seaside?
Mrs. Yuk, a young woman from Puryŏng, looked up at the sky
and wailed every night by the river.
Her husband lost his life last fall in a shipwreck off Hongwŏn
while he was carrying hwangjangmok.[185]
The governor falsely accused her husband of desertion
and tortured her in-laws for ten months.
It is said that Naesusa[186] didn't ask for hwanjangmok,
but the governor forged a royal command to fill his own belly.
Oh, heaven, heaven, do you know this or not?
Why don't you strike Governor Yu dead with lightning!

Yu Sangnyang forged a royal command to cut down one thousand hwangjangmok trees and ship them to him. But after the ship foundered off Hongwŏn, he bullied the sailors for the price of the trees. Hence people called him "Lord Hwangjangmok."

---

[185] The highest-quality pine, specially designated for the king's coffin.
[186] 內需司: The office in the royal palace in charge of supplying materials such as rice, clothes, labor, and miscellaneous things.

THINKING WINDOW VERSES

76. *Manho*[187] *Kang Sahŏn*

I ask, what do you think
of our beloved northern seaside?
Kang Sahŏn, the Manho of Ongnyŏn,[188]
was for generations a military clerk in P'ungsan.
Because he violated virgins and raped married women,
old men and children shed tears at the sound of crying in the village.
After bribing the Special Army Envoy with silver coins,
he behaved recklessly, like a whale.
Last fall, he made 100 nyang[189] selling people into slavery,
bought a horse at the market in Qing China, and offered it to the authorities.
How can I get hold of the executioner's sword
to cut off this wicked man's head?

Ongnyŏn is the name of a chin (鎭), a military post; its camp was in P'yemusan. Kang Sahŏn was originally a military official, but he bribed Ch'ae Pŏnam[190] *to secure a higher position, claiming he was of Chinese descent.*[191] *P'ungsan was the name of a chin.*

---

[187] The fourth-ranked military officer in charge of a chin, a provincial military post.
[188] A garrison in the Puryŏng regional military command, ruled by Manho.
[189] A unit of old Korean coinage; one nyang weighs about 37.3 grams.
[190] Ch'aejegong (1720-1799), a chief state councilor during King Chŏngjo's reign. Pŏnam was his penname; his other name was Paekkyu. He was the head of the Southerns.
[191] He seems to claim to be a descendant of Kang Sejak, a former military official of the Ming dynasty, who emigrated to

KIM RYŎ

77. *Censor Min Kihyŏn*

I ask, what do you think
of our beloved northern seaside?
Censor Min descends from the Lord of Yŏyang,[192]
brilliant, beautiful descendants continuing for generations.
I heard that when the Lord came as the censor, he fired corrupt officials,
encouraged righteousness, and rectified moral laws.
Pukkwan people still pass down "Eating Song for the Censor,"
bowing and praying when they cook.
Last winter a bad rumor about the censor circulated,
which came from the special army envoy.[193]
How can he pay his respects to the king's tomb,
when the elated spirits of Lord Munjŏng and Lord Ch'ungmun are still there?

After Lord Munjŏng Min Yujung rescued the northern people when he was the Kamjin Censor,[194] they wrote and sang "Eating Song for

Chosŭn and settled in Hoeryŏng, in neighboring Puryŏng.
[192] Min Yujung (1630-1687): A Confucian scholar and statesman. When his daughter married King Sukchong, he was appointed Lord of Yŏyang and later enshrined in King Hyojong's Tomb. His posthumous title is Lord Munjŏng.
[193] This seems to refer to Yi Pyŏngjŏng.
[194] The king's special censor sent to investigate famine-struck areas and rescue the hungry.

the Censor." The censor's name was Min Kihyŏn. [195] Lord Ch'ungmun was Chije Min Chinhu.

---

[195] Min Kihyŏn (1751-1811): A civil official in the late Chosŏn period. Because of his filial action, he was appointed mayor of Koch'ang. As the king's secret censor to Hamgyŏng Province in 1800, he reported on the mismanagement of eight towns, including Yi Chŏngman, magistrate of Kilchu.

78. Nam Ki'myŏng, a Merchant in Wŏnsan[196]

I ask, what do you think
of our beloved northern seaside?
Nam Ki'myŏng, a merchant in Wŏnsan,
was known as a flippant man of the world.
Holding the purple reins on his silver saddle,
he would travel to six military posts[197] and visit gisaeng houses.
One night in a Majo and Yukpak[198] card game
he bet five thousand strings of coin wrapped in silver cloth.
He lost his fortune, and now he runs a silver shop,
wears worn clothes and a smashed gat;[199] he doesn't loathe rice-bran gruel.
Nor has he mended his ways,
still exploiting people by secretly tipping off officials.

Yu Sangnyang opened a silver shop under Ch'ayuryŏng[200] for Nam Ki'myŏng to run, which led to great evil in the north, roiling both public and private worlds.

---

[196] A port city in South Hamgyŏng Province.
[197] Six garrisons in North Hamgyŏng Province: Kyŏngwŏn, Kyŏnghŭng, Hoeryŏng, Onsŏng, Jongsŏng, and Puryŏng.
[198] Mǎdiào (馬弔) and liùbó (六博) are Chinese card games.
[199] A traditional Korean hat made of bamboo and horsehair.
[200] A pass between Puryŏng County and Musan County in North Hamgyŏng Province.

THINKING WINDOW VERSES

79. Pŏsŏns[201]

I ask, what do you think
of our beloved northern seaside?
Last year, I changed my pŏsŏns three times a month.
This year I survived for nine months with one pair.
I remember Yŏnhŭi's hands sewing
the smooth finely threaded silk she bought in the Chinese market.
My new pŏsŏns' stitches were perfectly matched, like cucumber seeds;
her earnest love must have been wound into it.
Now I put on straw shoes;
my toes are chapped, my feet bare.
Why is it so agonizing to live?
I wander fields and ditches, cowering, my head bowed.

---

[201] Traditional Korean socks usually made of cotton.

KIM RYŎ

80. *My Eyeglasses*

I ask, what do you think
of our beloved northern seaside?
Crystal-like eyeglasses in a shark-skin case
bought in a market in Yanjing with one nip[202] of silver.
They were so bright, clear, and stainless
I could easily see things in the distance.
My cousin An sent them last year,
pitying my wandering and premature eye disease.
Mr. Kim, a petty official from Puryŏng Fortress, urged me
to trade my eyeglasses for his inferior ones.
Though his eyeglasses didn't work like Kyech'al's sword,[203]
I still tremble at the thought of them.

Northern people call eyeglasses glasses-eye. A nip of silver is a nyang. An is Academic An Ch'aek, my cousin by a paternal aunt. Kim Ibok was the name of a petty official, now dead.

---

[202] Traditional unit of counting flat things like coins and straw bags.

[203] 季札 Jizha: An expression of regret for an unfulfilled friendship. When Lord Jizha of Wu, traveling as an envoy, met the King of Xu, he sensed the king wanted his sword. But he planned to give it to him on his way home, by which time the king was dead. So he visited his tomb and placed his sword in the bough of a tree.

THINKING WINDOW VERSES

81. *An Ink Stick from Nanjing*

I ask, what do you think
of our beloved northern seaside?
This tributary ink stick from Nanjing, imprinted with Pangwhan,²⁰⁴
was circular in shape and called P'umjungnandae.²⁰⁵
When ground, it neither clotted nor spread;
rich and mellow, it shone dark red like ochre lacquer.
Congealing purple ripples released the fragrance of musk,
and when I dipped my brush in, a black bubble spilled out.
I cherished it, never used it carelessly,
and only wrote out a phrase of *Yaksong*²⁰⁶ as Ŭngya did.
Heaven produced a rare masterpiece, which people threw away.
I fear that good works will disappear from the literary world.

Yun'in²⁰⁷ gave me a tributary ink stick made by Cho Panghwan from the Qing dynasty. Its name was P'umjungnandae (品重蘭臺).

---

²⁰⁴ 方寰 Fanghuan: Refers to Cao Fanghuan 曹方寰.
²⁰⁵ 品重蘭臺 Pinshonglantai means high-quality; lantai was the name of the court library in the Han dynasty; this ink stick was thus used in the royal court.
²⁰⁶ 藥誦 Yaosong, *Medicine: A Text by Su Shi* 蘇軾. This book argues that people should not excessively pursue or refuse the five tastes but eat food in tune with one's health.
²⁰⁷ Kim Chosun's penname.

82. Kim Choi,[208] My Neighbor Woman

I ask, what do you think
of our beloved northern seaside?
Despicable was Kim Choi, my neighbor to the south.
There was such a woman[209] in Hagan, and now the same
   one is here.
Rough-skinned, with a bluish mien, she walks like a duck.
She had pemphigus as a girl, which weakened her voice
and let three husbands go in a month, as if plucking her
   eyebrows.
Even during national mourning, she gave in to envy.
She was promiscuous as a beast.
At last prostitution came to Kwanbuk:[210]
the dark rumor about Lord Yu spread around the world.

Puryŏng Fortress's seal clerk, Kim Sŏkch'u's sister was promiscuous. Petty official Kim Sangguk and Cho Ikwan were Kim's cousins, who slandered each other because of Kim Choi. She was sentenced to slavery for her sins, while Yu Sangnyang collected ransom.

---

208 召史: The title after one's surname used to indicate a commoner's wife or widow.
209 A woman in 河間 Hejian means a promiscuous woman. In 柳宗元 Liu Zongyuan's *The Story of Heijian*, she is a chaste woman, who was seduced by a relative, then indulged herself, ruining her body.
210 The area north of Mach'ŏllŏng Pass, another name for North Hamgyŏng Province.

THINKING WINDOW VERSES

83. *Jade Water-Dropper*

I ask, what do you think
of our beloved northern seaside?
A yellow jade water-dropper with black dots
carved by a master artisan from Hunyung.[211]
The front is taller than its crouching back and axillaries.
Water comes in and out through the open holes,
the one behind for swallowing and spitting up water.
It looks like a real toad, full of life.
It has its own long history:
Yi Yŏngik used it first before giving it to Tamsu.[212]
I traded it for my ivory brush stand
carved by Sangjwa and kept it on my desk.

Hunyung is the name of a garrison where jade artisans worked. I had an ivory brush stand carved by Pak Sangjwa.

---

[211] A village by the border of Onsŏng-kun, Hamgyŏng Province, on the Yulu River's southern shore.
[212] The penname of Pak Kyŏngsil, whose other name was Sŏngsin. He was Kim Ryŏ's student.

KIM RYŎ

84. *Eight Folds of Pictures*

I ask, what do you think
of our beloved northern seaside?
The folds include a picture of a pavilion with a bamboo
   forest and water-shield plants
and a sudden gust of clear wind, which cleans and refreshes.
There are also mountains, rivers, a flowering Japanese
   apricot, and chrysanthemums.
It is composed of eight folds, including the picture of
   bamboo.
Sŏngsin[213] deceived me, borrowing it, like Hyŏngju,[214]
and Hŭiik[215] chimed in, like Nosuk.[216]
Konso[217] just watched, like Chegallyang.[218]
Who won the power play between Son Kwŏn[219] and Yu

---

[213] Pak Kyŏngsil's penname—Tamsu was his other name. He was a petty official in the barracks. See #36.

[214] After the Battle of Red Cliff, the seven provinces of 荊州 Jingzhou were occupied by Liu Bei, Cao Cao, and Sun Quan. Liu Bei, geographically disadvantaged, asked Sun Quan to loan him the southern Jingzhou, thus securing five provinces and laying the foundation for Shuhan. Hence "Lie Bei borrowed Jingzhou" came to mean "not to return what one has borrowed."

[215] Kim Hyŏng'yu's other name. He was Kim Ryŏ's student. See #5.

[216] 魯肅 Lu Su: A military general and politician serving under the warlord Sun Quan during the late Eastern Han dynasty.

[217] Nam Hŭng'yu's other name. He was a fine calligrapher. See #9.

[218] 諸葛亮 Zhuge Liang: His other name was Kongming. He was a military strategist and writer in the Eastern Han dynasty.

[219] 孫權 Sun Quan: His other name was Zhongmou. He was the founder of the state of Eastern Wu during the Three Kingdoms

Pi?[220]
This is how gains and losses go in human affairs.
How can I claim it's mine, when he borrowed it for so long?

---

period.
[220] 劉備 Liu Bei: His courtesy name was Xuande. A warlord in the late Eastern Han dynasty, he founded the state of Shu Han.

85. *A Pair of Ivory Brush Stands*

I ask, what do you think
of our beloved northern seaside?
Pieces of red and green ivory as soft as jade.
I bought a pair from an interpreter who frequented Yanjing.
With a sharp knife, Chŏnjwa carved each letter quickly,
delicately. He copied out three chapters of "Ch'ŏngp'-
   yŏngsa,"[221]
then added flowing water and blue mountains.
Meanwhile, Tamsu returned my red brush stand.
I keep the remaining one in my bookcase.
Surely there is time for divine things to be united.
How can we leave them buried in the mud?

Chŏnjwa is Sangjwa; his name is Pak Kyŏmjin, and his other name is Ch'iik. As noted above, he was good at carving letters with a sharp knife.

---

[221] 清平詞 Qingping Tune: Li Bai's poem celebrating the beauty of Yang Qui Fei.

THINKING WINDOW VERSES

86. *I Met Yŏnhŭi in a Dream*

I ask, what do you think
of our beloved northern seaside?
I dreamed tonight in an inn, under a lonely oil lamp,
that I went into Yŏnhŭi's house to play in the pavilion.
She was standing alone by the western banister,
her head bowed, her eyebrows anxious.
The China pink flowers on the stone steps were gone,
doves were crying in pairs.
When I climbed the ladder to the pavilion
and called her to bring wine, she ignored me.
When I woke, only the early morning moon was shining.

87. *Sir Yuchŏng's "Pugŏ Poems"*

I ask, what do you think
of our beloved northern seaside?
Sir Yujŏng[222] was a masterful writer,
and I pity his miserable wandering until he was middle-aged.
When I read his *Pugŏ Poems*,[223]
they are as dynamic and grand as the writings of Han Toeji.[224]
His calligraphy is like that of Cho Maengbu;[225]
the Chinese ink remains clear and brilliant to this day.
Though he suffered terribly in the universal conflagration,
the misfortune regarding his writings was more shocking,
    because unexpected.
Scholar Ch'a[226] did not betray me—I betrayed him.
I am too ashamed even to grieve.

---

[222] Yujŏng was the penname of Yi Yŏng'ik, who followed his father into exile in Puryŏng. An outstanding scholar and calligrapher, he did not seek a government position and died at forty.
[223] Pugŏ is Puryŏng's other name.
[224] 韓退之 Han Tuizhi: The other name of Han Yu (768 – 824), a Tang dynasty writer, poet, and government official, who shaped the development of Neo-Confucianism. Described as "comparable in stature to Dante, Shakespeare or Goethe" for his influence on Chinese letters, he is widely considered to be one of China's finest prose writers.
[225] 趙孟頫 Zhao Mengfu: A descendant of the Song dynasty's imperial family and a scholar, painter and calligrapher during the Yuan dynasty.
[226] See #1.

THINKING WINDOW VERSES

Yuchŏng wrote fifty Pugŏ Poems, *which Ch'a Namgyu kept in his house. I borrowed it to read, but when I was arrested, my documents were confiscated, including the book.*

88. *Noh Simhong, a Gisaeng in Tohobu*

I ask, what do you think
of our beloved northern seaside?
The girl from the Noh family was fifteen years old,
charming, a fine singer and dancer.
She had the face of an apricot flower, a willow-thin waist,
and the sweet voice of a golden oriole.
Drinking rules[227] were strict at night in the high pavilion,
but the moonlight on the banisters was silky.
Her smooth, fragrant skin was reflected
in the apricot chŏgsam dappled with patterns.
When she sang "Kwansannagmaehwa,"[228]
the heart of an exile from the south melted.

Noh Simhong, a gisaeng in Tohobu, was a legendary beauty, singer, and Korean zither player. A relative of Yŏnhŭi, she was an expert in drinking rules. I wrote "A Short Story of Simhong's Life" separately.

---

[227] The rules for a drinking party agreed to by the participants.
[228] 關山落梅花: The title of the song means "apricot flowers fall on the border."

89. *Kwŏn Chong'il's Calligraphy*

I ask, what do you think
of our beloved northern seaside?
Kwŏn Chong'il, my junior but a man to be respected,
is already better in chirography than Pak Kyŏngsil.[229]
His strokes are thin but firm, his style grand,
but his uncle was more enthusiastic.
Kwŏn stayed alone in the Kangsin Temple last winter
and reduced five hundred white brushes to stubs.
Nanjŏng style[230] has lately gotten weird.
Who best imitated it? Tong T'aesa.[231]
Chong'il was Tong's most faithful follower.
Why don't you sell his works in the market in Yanjing?

Kwŏn Chong'il's other name was Paekham. He was a clerk at the army base and a fine calligrapher. His uncle Ch'ungguk's other name was Yuryang. The Kangsin temple is twenty li south of town.

---

[229] See #36.

[230] 蘭亭 Lanting: Refers to Lantingxu (蘭亭序), Wang Xizhi's semi-cursive style of calligraphy, which he used in 353; a representative Chinese calligraphy made into a copybook.

[231] 董太史: Refers to 董其昌 Dong Qichang (1555-1636), a Ming dynasty painter, scholar, calligrapher, and art theorist.

90. *Hwajŏn[232] Outing*

I ask, what do you think
of our beloved northern seaside?
Spring had returned to the Karigol valley
and a thousand splendid azaleas opened.
Yŏnhŭi planned a hwajŏn outing
and sent a memo on Kyujŏn paper[233] inviting me to join her.
Her younger sister Simhong and Miss Yang also came,
Simhong brought Nokkigŭm[234] and Yang, a drum.
We sat on fallen petals at the secluded edge
of a deep stream and surrendered to pleasure.
When the sunset spread and the crescent moon rose,
we came back singing and chanting before separating.

The valley is west of town. Miss Yang is Kwanok, Yŏnhŭi's cousin.

---

[232] Pan-fried sweet rice cake decorated with flower petals.
[233] A type of paper made from dew-wet rose mallow leaves pressed into juice and applied to paper, which dries with rocks on top. It is said that the renowned Chinese poet Bai Jui only used this paper.
[234] 綠綺琴 Luqiqin, Green Dragonfly Zither: The name bestowed by the zither player Liang Wang on Sima Xiangru in the Han dynasty when the poet offered him "Jade Fu 玉如意賦," which means a common zither.

THINKING WINDOW VERSES

91. *Toho Yi Kan's Grave*

I ask, what do you think
of our beloved northern seaside?
A four-foot-tall grave on Chŏngt'amnyŏng Pass,
where Toho Yi was said to have been buried long ago.
When barbarians from over the border, bandit boars and snakes,
invaded our northern territory, they aimed for critical points.
When a thousand soldiers were killed and the bandits ran wilder yet,
Toho had only one spear left.
He fought to the end of his life but what could he do alone?
His spirit of fidelity did not die.
Whenever it is cloudy, his soul seems to cry;
desolate skeletons are scattered around this valley.

Chŏngt'amnyŏng Pass is west of town. Barbarians at the border invaded our country in 1600, killing Toho Yi in the war. I wrote Details of Toho Yi's Death in the War *separately.*

92. *Miserable Mrs. Nam*

I ask, what do you think
of our beloved northern seaside?
Mrs. Nam of Yŏnch'ŏn was miserable indeed.
Her grudges reached Hades and would not dissolve.
"My in-laws are virtuous and respectable,
but my fate as a daughter-in-law is unfortunate.
I can endure even if my fingers are cut off and my brain
 bursts.
What grieves me is that my legacy will be infamy."
In a flash her blood dyed the river forever red,
as if petals fluttered on it.
I only hope her soul becomes a wild grudging ghost
that kills every descendant of the Yu family in the world.

The daughter-in-law of Nam Chein, a rich man in Yŏnch'ŏn, was a woman whose maiden name was Chŏng. Her grandmother-in-law killed her. An investigation began, which Yu Sangnyang stopped after her father-in-law bribed him.

THINKING WINDOW VERSES

93. On Yŏnhŭi's Birthday

I ask, what do you think
of our beloved northern seaside?
Silk-like snow fell lightly on January 25th—
Yŏnhŭi's birthday.
New wine from a silver kettle was poured into a jade cup,
fragrant ripples of pearl splashing in the wine jar.
Rice-cake soup warmed our stomachs cooled by han'gu,[235]
followed by another soup of golden pheasant and then a
   lamb dish.
I know how dearly elder Chang and Pak love their children.
What gift did I bring her? A beautiful jade norigae.[236]
"My beloved, please get dead drunk today,
and don't show me your anxious face."

Yŏnhŭi invited Kukpo and Kyŏngsil to her birthday party and asked me to drink with them so that I would be freed from my anxiety.

---

[235] An oil-and-honey pastry, eaten as an appetizer before breakfast.
[236] Traditional ornaments worn by Korean women.

94. Merciless Yi Pyŏngjŏng

I ask, what do you think
of our beloved northern seaside?
A thousand kil of snow fell on Mach'ŏllyŏng Pass
and all traffic to the north was halted.
This morning there was a sudden uproar in town.
The director of the state tribunal and a high-ranking official arrived.
The schedule was tight, his voice loud as thunder,
the king had exiled Minister Sŏ[237] to the north.
Rumor had it the assistant prefect of Hamhŭng had sent him wine and meat.
The chief border inspector slandered him, caught him out, arrested him,
shocking the townspeople, who dared not ask
why he came one evening to a house south of the Fortress, begging for food.

When Lord Sŏ Yurin was exiled to Kyŏnghŭng, Hamhŭng assistant prefect Kim Kip'ung sent him wine and meat. Yi Pyŏngjŏng fired him for communicating with a sinner.

---

[237] Sŏ Yurin (1783-1802), a statesman of the late Chosŏn period, was the Inspector General and Minister of Defense.

THINKING WINDOW VERSES

95. *The Unstable Political Situation in Seoul*

I ask, what do you think
of our beloved northern seaside?
The news from Seoul: people feel alienated from the
  government.
This spring, I was surprised three times by messengers
  from the Royal Court.
Lord Sŏ and Lord Yi's carriages moved north,
and Kongse crossed the Kwimun'gwan Gateway.[238]
I heard a rumor that Tamjŏng[239] would be put to death;
day and night he stared at the southern sky, hungry for a
  heavenly blessing.
I didn't write "Hanjŏngbu;"[240]
stainless jade suffers envy for no reason at all.
Oh heaven, there must be time to repent!
Why should I have to remain in prison until death?

---

[238] A gateway to Kyŏngsŏng, Hamgyŏng Province: a place from which it is difficult to return alive.
[239] Kim Ryŏ's penname.
[240] In 閒情賦 "Xianquing Fu," Tao Yuanming sings of his desire to live in retirement—which prompted Xia Tong of the Liang dynasty to say, "Among all his works, only 'Xianquing Fu' is like a stain on jade."

Minister Yi Chaehak²⁴¹ was living in exile in Onsŏng. Scholar Kim Ikyo²⁴² 's other name was Kongse; he was exiled to Myŏngch'ŏn. Rumors also landed me in prison.

---

²⁴¹ Yi Chehak (1745 -1806): A civil official in the late Chosŏn period. When King Sunjo ascended to the throne in 1800, he was exiled to Kasan then relocated to Onsŏng the next year.
²⁴² Kim Ikyo (1764 – 1806): A civil official in the late Chosŏn period. His other name was Kongse. A member of the Party of Expediency exiled to Myŏngch'ŏn by the Party of Principle in 1800.

THINKING WINDOW VERSES

96. *Wino[243] Went to Buy Herring*

I ask, what do you think
of our beloved northern seaside?
Ravens had been cawing since dawn,
lots of herring would be caught.
After I sent Wino to Sŏra to buy herring,
I worried because he did not return for three days.
Suddenly, a child ran up to me shouting, "Wino is back!"
I saw a load of herring piled neatly on the horse.
I ran to him in joy, held the reins,
clasped his hand: "How was your journey?"
He replied, "Good, good." But he was about to cry,
anxious about my health. He said I did not look well.

Sŏra is a western port in Kyŏngsŏng, where the house of Pijang Yi Chungbae can be found. The people in Pukkwan say that if ravens cover the sky, it is a sign that herring will be caught. It is especially true around Kyŏngch'ip.[244]

---

[243] Kim Ryŏ's personal servant.
[244] One of the twenty-four seasonal divisions, which begins on March 5th—the day when insects emerge from the earth.

97. *The Brushes I Made*

I ask, what do you think
of our beloved northern seaside?
Old Man Pak of Musan gave me a wicker basket
with three hundred weasel tails to make hairbrushes.
I sent my servant Wi to Kyŏngsŏng to buy bamboo for the handles.
There was also a box of bamboo my caretaker collected separately.
I added other hairs, made some required works,
and tied thirty solid color brushes without tips in every bundle.
I planned to send half to Sŏwŏn
and use the other half with my students.
Waste resulting from mismanagement is laughable.
What a pity to tie them into bundles and not use them.

The man from Musan was Pak Ch'anggyŏng. He was my landlord's father-in-law, Sŏ Undae, who hunted martens. My students, including Kang Ŭng'a, read books that winter in the village school.

THINKING WINDOW VERSES

98. *On Publishing* Ch'anggaru's Unofficial History[245] *and Other Books*

I ask, what do you think
of our beloved northern seaside?
Naksu transcribed *Ch'anggaru's Unofficial History*
and *Yuninkwan's Unofficial History* in characters small as flies.
Tamsu's copy was crude,
Ŭng'ya's, delicate.
I tried to borrow the original *Yuninkwan's Unofficial History*
   from Tŏkham—
a pious man, who safeguarded it.
A thousand-li-deep steep valley found in a foot of flat land.
The things of the world change and turn, like tangled
   threads.
When news arrived like a thunderbolt, I was at a loss.
How could I complain about my situation in trivial letters?

Naksu, my distant grandson-like family member, copied Ch'anggaru's Unofficial History, *which I collected and edited, and Vice Minister Kim Chosun's* Yuninkwan's Unofficial History. *Tŏkham is a young man whose other name is Manyong.*

---

[245] An unofficial history collected and edited by Kim Ryŏ. Manuscripts of five unofficial histories were handed down. In the preface to *Ch'anggaru Unofficial's History*, we learn the book originally contained seven unofficial histories.

99. *Clothes Yŏnhŭi Made for Me*

I ask, what do you think
of our beloved northern seaside?
When rain fell occasionally during the long summer,
Yŏnhŭi wove hemp cloth in Chakyŏnsa—
one hundred cha in four days and two more days at that pace;
the cloth was fine as silk, almost transparent.
With two p'ils[246] of cloth, she made a ceremonial robe and gown,
and then another p'il for a vest and a lined jacket.
She used one p'il and ten chas of cloth to make unlined trousers.
She even made a ch'ang'ŭi,[247] a sleeveless jacket and leggings.
With her own hands, Yŏnhŭi made
a new set of clothes for this old man's body.

In Yŏnhŭi's house was a weaving room I named Chakyŏnsa (翛然舍) on my signboard. Puggwan people always weave linen cloth when it rains. One p'il is thirty-five chas.

---

[246] A traditional unit of measuring cloth. One p'il is thirty-five cha, one cha is 30.3 cm, so one p'il is about 4.5 m.
[247] A jacket worn by governmental officials.

THINKING WINDOW VERSES

100. *Mr. Kim, a Brush Maker*

I ask, what do you think
of our beloved northern seaside?
There are two master brush makers in the north:
Mr. Ch'oe is old, and Mr. Kim is young.
Kim is agile, marvelously skilled,
with mutton-chop sideburns and a quick hand.
Seated on a cushion with a lit lamp on a quiet night,
he ties hairs evenly without a break.
When I went to the Pukye Market last winter,
he saw me off at the stream, holding a bottle of rice wine.
He gave me a broom-sized white brush,
which I kept in a book box. I haven't used it yet.

Mr. Ch'oe's name is Taeyŏn, and Mr. Kim's is Tŏkch'ae. Both are master brush makers. Pukye is a placename in Chongsŏng.

KIM RYŎ

101. *In Memory of Minister Chŏng Chonjung*

I ask, what do you think
of our beloved northern seaside?
Alack and alas! Minster Chŏng of Chunam
loved me like a son or a cousin,
and when I heard he had passed away last fall,
I wept in silence, tears streaking my beard.
The sky was high that day and a cold wind blew
as I rushed to the blue river to cry.
I still remember the night of unmelted snow
when we climbed joyfully to the Kongbungnu Pavilion to
    greet each other.
Our cups overflowed with fine wine from a silver kettle,
    like river water;
the moon like a bow hung above the silky Kŭmgang River.

Chunam is a placename in Kyŏnggi Province. The Lord's name was Chŏng Chonjung, and his other name was Sajŏng. I received his friendship and benevolence. When he was the governor of Hosŏ Province, we lingered in the Kongbungnu Pavilion.

102. *Yŏngsanok's Note*

I ask, what do you think
of our beloved northern seaside?
The autumn drizzle went on for ten days.
I closed the door, lamenting my loneliness, like sick Chasang.[248]
Yŏngsanok sent a steamed chicken with a note
and new wine clear as crystal in a jade-green bottle.
"When the rain stops and the moon shines,
I will wait for you with Aunt Noh,
Sister Yu, and Sister Chi at the south end of the Yŏngnakchŏng Pavilion
and the western bank of the Hwakyo Bridge.
We will bring the geomungo and the green flute.
You don't have to prepare turtle soup and filleted raw carp.
Wine flows like an ocean in my house."

Yŏngsanok, a gisaeng for the Pu, was a fine poet, singer, and geomungo performer. She was paesuch'ŏp[249] of Sirang[250] Sŏ. She called me "Ajubeonim,"[251] because we were related.

---

[248] 子桑 Zisang: A fictitious character in *Zuangzi*, who laments his fate, locked inside for ten days of heavy rain.
[249] 配修妾: A woman who cares for an exile.
[250] The title of a government position equivalent to vice minister.
[251] The title of a husband's older brother.

103. *To See Yŏnhŭi at the End of the Rainy Season*

I ask, what do you think
of our beloved northern seaside?
Because the stream flooded during the long summer rain,
I haven't seen Yŏnhŭi's face for five days.
Today the rain stopped, the moon rose over the sandbar,
and the willows on the shore fluttered like green silk gauze.
I put on my hemp shoes, walked out with my cane toward
 the shore,
and absently turned toward Yŏnhŭi's house.
Then I saw swaying tree boughs, and a shadow flashed
 across
the thick forest on the sandbank.
Holding her tiny parasol and a bottle of wine,
Yŏnhŭi, wearing a hemp skirt, was coming across the
 bridge.

THINKING WINDOW VERSES

104. *My Cousin, An Ch'aek*²⁵²

I ask, what do you think
of our beloved northern seaside?
Academician An is my generous cousin,
who was appointed censor of the Qing Market this winter.
From the empress tree by the bamboo fence
I was watching a procession of swaying silk parasols from the south,
when I recognized him by his old bearing.
We clasped hands and cried and then fell silent.
There were snow flurries in the air, and the north wind howled sadly.
When he stopped at a stone grave in Immyŏng,²⁵³ he said,
he saw my forty-character poem
inscribed on the white-plaster wall of Sir Cho's²⁵⁴ shrine,
where the blood stains are still innocently red.

*When I was exiled to the north, I paid my respects at Chungbong Sir Cho's shrine, and wrote a poem on the wall, which is recorded in Kamdam Journal.*²⁵⁵

---

²⁵² An Ch'aek (1742 - ?): A civil official in the late Chosŏn period. His other name was Chisuk. He passed the civil service examination in 1775 and was a secretary in the Ministry of Military Affairs and Yangju County Magistrate. He was Kim Ryŏ's cousin.
²⁵³ A placename in North Hamgyŏng Province.
²⁵⁴ Refers to Cho Hŏn, a Confucian scholar and general in a volunteer army. Chungbong was his penname; Yŏsik was his other name. He fought the Japanese army and died at Kŭmsan, along with seven hundred troops.
²⁵⁵ Kim Ryŏ's journal recording his exile and the details of his journey to Puryŏng.

105. *After Meeting An Kwangjik, Cousin An's Nephew*

I ask, what do you think
of our beloved northern seaside?
This evening, I saw An Chubaek face to face,
smiling, five years after our separation.
Sitting close enough for our knees to touch, we burst into tears,
it felt as if we were in a dream.
I heard you study as hard as ever, while my hair turns grey.
I study your face, holding the dying lamplight.
You tell me that in my village in the Kahoe district[256]
Ta'kyŏng passed away; also Kyŏngsŏn.
I suppose that only white herons fly for very long
above the Paengnowŏn garden,[257] near the Hamch'wi Pavilion.[258]

Cousin An's nephew, Kwangjik's other name is Chubaek. Kahoe is a district name. Hong Ingmun Ta'kyŏng and Hong Talyŏng Kyŏngsŏn were my classmates.

---

[256] One of ten districts in northern Seoul during the Chosŏn period.
[257] A garden constructed by Maeng Mant'aek, a civil official during the reign of King Sukchong. Kim Ryŏ notes that his house was located west of the garden. The literal meaning of Paengnowŏn is "a garden for white herons."
[258] A pavilion at Kim Ryŏ's house in Samch'ŏng-dong.

THINKING WINDOW VERSES

106. *Yŏnhŭi's Words of Warning*

I ask, what do you think
of our beloved northern seaside?
Yŏnhŭi warned me to be careful in what I write,
"You're liable to meet disaster in this chaotic world."
Staying up all night, wrapped in a cold comforter,
we talked about things old and new, wiping away our tears.
The snow stopped that day, but the wind stayed strong;
moonlight filled the cloudless sky, like a lake.
Now I hear dry leaves falling in the yard
and lament our parting so soon after meeting.
Separated like a northern swallow and a southern goose at
   the corners of the sky,
who can I tell about my aching heart?

107. *After Suffering Calamities*

I ask, what do you think
of our beloved northern seaside?
Three days of typhoon brought down rocks and houses,
blowing sand and pebbles, uprooting tall trees.
The anxious old men Pak and Kang sighed:
"We must cry out, because we have the 'Hwasan' [259]
    divination sign."
I said, "We suffered unexpected calamites from heaven.
How can I follow a lofty scholar from Wu?"[260]
Not long ago, eating in the south, my anger flared up again.
Who could imagine this would become a prediction?
Heaven determines one's prosperity and downfall.
What use is there in complaining about fate?

I built a hut on a small patch of land under the rock and named it "Hwat'ang."[261] *But it was uprooted by high winds last winter. A local clerk, Pak, was good at reading divinatory signs. Mr. Kang Tŏngni is Ŭng'ya's father.*

---

[259] The sign for "burning mountain and boiling sea," i.e., something urgent and dangerous.

[260] If the Shaowei star (少微星) shines, a secluded scholar returns to the world; when it loses light, the scholar dies. When the reclusive scholar Xie Fu at Huiji of Dongjin lived on Ruoye Mountain, the moon suddenly eclipsed the star. Because Dai Kui of Wu was better known than Xie Fu, people said, "Isn't this a sign that Dai Kui will die?" but it was Xie Fu who died soon after. To make fun of someone from Wu, people say, "The lofty scholar of Wu will not die even if he wants to."

[261] Literally, a house in a birch forest in which one cultivates a vigorous spirit.

THINKING WINDOW VERSES

108. *Sŏryŏm's Tweezers*

I ask, what do you think
of our beloved northern seaside?
A lovely pair of tiny, silver-plated copper tweezers,
all the dearer because a pretty woman gave them to me.
I got dead drunk at Chŏng Sŏryŏm's house,
which is just outside Kwanghwamun, [262] west of the Sŏkkyo Bridge.
She took out her tweezers and put them in my hand,
I rewarded her with a pure golden comb.
She is dead, and since I cannot meet her again
I touch the tweezers day and night with tears in my eyes.
Now even the tweezers are gone
and tears roll down my cheeks.

Sŏryŏm was a gisaeng in the region of Kwansŏ.[263] *I wrote* The Story of Chŏng Sŏryŏm *and her epitaph. Yŏnhŭi wrote* Noesa.[264]

---

[262] The name of the Fortress Gate in Puryŏng.
[263] West of Mach'ollyŏng Pass, in P'yŏngan Province, and north of Hwanghae Province.
[264] A text praising the virtuous deeds of a dead person.

109. *Unfinished* Collection of Stories of Famous Korean Statesmen

I ask, what do you think
of our beloved northern seaside?
Editing *A Collection of Stories of Famous Korean Statesmen*,
I foolishly compared mine with Chu Un'gok.[265]
I devoted myself to this book for ten years,
barely finishing the introduction, tables, and names—
just a spindle turning with gentle words and strict judgment.
I didn't forget those gentlemen's true pictures even while I ate.
Last fall, Scholar Hong volunteered to help with the variorum edition,
and Scholar Nam wanted to proofread the book.
What use is it to spend half of my life working on this!
When I look to the north, my heart grows uneasy.

Scholar Hong of Puryŏng is Kisŏk, a great Confucian scholar whose other name is Sŏngsa. Scholar Nam is Hŭng'yu.

---

[265] Refers to Zhu Xi, who edited *A Collection of Stories of Famous Statesmen from the Song Dynasty*—required reading for Chosŏn dynasty politicians. Un'gok was his student in Fujiansheng.

THINKING WINDOW VERSES

110. *Sangch'ŏl and T'aeyo, Yi Kwangsa's Students*

I ask, what do you think
of our beloved northern seaside?
Only a few students from Wŏnkyo remain,
among them, Pang Sangch'ŏl and Kim T'aeyo.
Elder Pang is loyal to the king and a learned scholar,
while upright Kim is not bad at learning.
Both honor their teacher's example;
metaphorically speaking, they're the best of the bunch.
When I met two old people, my thoughts turned dark
and we drank a lot, talking about the past.
I'm as stupid as a deaf blindman,
ashamed of my failure to reach the heights of the former exile.

Sangch'ŏl's other name is Kunch'ŭk. His brother Sanghŭp's other name is Yŏhwa. He won first prize in the military service examination and was an upright man.

KIM RYŎ

111. *Chimok, Son of Sir Yujŏng*

I ask, what do you think
of our beloved northern seaside?
Born six months after me,
Sir Yujŏng's son was named Chimok.
He is naïve, stubborn, gloomy,
and illiterate, with disheveled hair and jagged sideburns.
It seems that Sir Yujŏng did not name him randomly.
I wonder what kind of woman delivered such a baby.
His ancestors are famous, but his family is ruined.
He married a daughter from the Chu family.
Fortunately, his descendants were not cut off.
Nor will he fret about his son's talents or lifespan.

The daughter of the Chu family is Kapnom, who is from Seoul. When she was three years old, her father committed a crime and was exiled here. Chimok married her.

THINKING WINDOW VERSES

112. *Because I Wrote* The Life of Chŏngan[266]

I ask, what do you think
of our beloved northern seaside?
Not taking Yŏnhŭi's advice,
I wrote *The Life of Chŏngan* without a second thought.
How could I know it would lead to disaster,
with a mad hound barking out serious charges?
He closed the gates to the castle and arrested people at midnight,
shouting and bludgeoning them.
Many men vomited blood and women had nosebleeds.
I touched the tiger's nostril hairs and fell prey to its hunger.
I regret—in vain—brandishing my three-inch tongue.
Thinking this over late at night, I feel deep shame.

Because Yŏngsanok remained loyal to Sirang Sŏ, Yu Sangnyang had people arrested. I wrote about this in The Life of Chŏngan. *Infuriated, Yu investigated* The Criminal Case of Kim Chongwŏn.

---

[266] Chŏngan means "a goose keeping faith," since geese mate for life. Kim Ryŏ seems to have written this piece mindful of Yŏngsanok, who stayed loyal to Vice Director Sŏ.

113. *My Lost Writings*

I ask, what do you think
of our beloved northern seaside?
If Usan's misfortune was that his Kang'unnu Pavilion burned down,[267]
Chongwŏn's imprisonment[268] was a joke.
The sky was pale, the sun, dark blue with looming disaster;
the lingering fragrance and oil[269] vanished in a flash.
After the fire, I still have forty books—
how can I complain about brushstrokes weakened by muddy ink?
The owner of the Ch'ŏnyŏngnu Pavilion[270] treasured what I had,
having copied out my books on clean paper and bound them with white silk.
Now the books are gone: silverfish following in my footsteps
have turned my writings into white ash.

---

[267] Usan refers to Qian Qian Li (錢謙益), a literary figure and statesman of the Ming and Qing dynasties, who helped write the history of the Ming. After his death, Emperor Qianlong accused him of disloyalty, and all the woodblocks of his texts were burned. His library, the Kang'unnu Pavilion (絳雲樓), had tens of thousands of books.

[268] See # 112.

[269] This refers to poetry composed with great effort. 元稹 Yuan Zhen in the Tang dynasty, praising Du Fu's poems, said "the lingering fragrance and oil will benefit poets to come."

[270] Refers to Yŏnhŭi.

THINKING WINDOW VERSES

Kim Chongwŏn is Sanggi's son; his other name is Naehyŏng. Slandered by Yu Sangnyang, he was flogged then exiled. That was when my books were burned, as I wrote in A Book of Thousand Worries and Ten Thousand Grudges (千愁萬恨書).

114. The Spirit of P'ach'ong[271] Chang

I ask, what do you think
of our beloved northern seaside?
How dignified is the spirit of P'ach'ong Chang.
He regards snobs like worms.
He keeps Wŏnkyo's poems on his desk
to admire and recite day and night.
He adjusts his clothes and kneels as if to face the king—
he is someone who truly respects his teacher.
He always says, "After meeting the teacher Wŏnkyo,
all mountains except T'aesan[272] look like hills."
Who drops gravel into a clean well?
He alone is virtuous in this rough world.

P'ach'ong Chang's name is Hyŏllyŏng; his other name is Hukyo. He studied under Wŏnkyo. His sister was Wŏnkyo's mistress. I wrote The Life of Chang Hyŏllyŏng *and* Chang Aeae Poems *separately.*

---

[271] 把摠: The fourth-ranked military official in a military camp.
[272] 泰山 Taishan: Mt. Tai is a mountain of historical and cultural significance north of the city of Tai'an, in Shandong Province, China.

THINKING WINDOW VERSES

115. *After Meeting Yi Sago*

I ask, what do you think
of our beloved northern seaside?
Yi Sago was an exile in Myŏngch'ŏn,
who had the same great-great-grandfather as Yi Yŏngik.
The dark wart in the middle of his forehead was as large
    as a gadfly;
his eyes were the color of autumn water shining brilliantly.
Under Tobo,[273] he learned calligraphy, succeeding in the
    family tradition,
and shocked the world with his writing, surpassing Wang
    Uch'ing.[274]
Even if he suffered nine deaths at the border, it would not
    shake his loyalty.
He drank and talked, slapping his hands.
When our talk turned to the factions caused by the
    argument
between Hoech'on and Yubong,[275] he waved his arms,
    growing indignant.

---

[273] The other name of Yi Kwangsa, a renowned calligrapher of the late Chosŏn period.

[274] 王禹偁 Wang Yucheng: A famous poet (954-1001) in the North Song dynasty.

[275] A series of arguments between the disciples of Hoech'ŏn and Yubong, which eventually led them to split into two factions, Old Doctrine and Young Doctrine. Hoech'on was the penname of Song Siyŏl, and Yubong was the penname of Yun Chŭng. Yi Sago's family belonged to Young Doctrine, while Kim Ryŏ's family belonged to the Old Doctrine.

KIM RYŎ

Sago's name is Myŏnsi. I spent a night with him at Kyŏngsil's house. I wrote "A Poem for Wine and Song" and gave it to him.

THINKING WINDOW VERSES

116. *Missing Puryŏng*

I ask, what do you think
of our beloved northern seaside?
I lived in Puryŏng for only five years,
but I think about it day and night.
I'm going crazy longing for it;
my heart and bowels feel like they were sliced open.
Even in dream, my soul wanders through elderly Sŏ's house,
where I lived, south of Murŭng and west of Mt. Ullyong.
If my brief love under the mulberry tree[276] is like this,
how much dearer is Seoul where I was raised.
A year comes to a close, but I miss both even more.
The heart of an exile sitting in a dark room aches.

Mt. Ullyong is Mt. Ch'ŏnggye, and Murŭng is the name of its pass.

---

[276] The phrase means he cannot forget this relationship, brief as it was. It alludes to "襄楷列傳 Xaingkai Liezhuan" in 後漢書 *Book of the Late Han*: "The monk studying Buddhism does not stay three nights in a row under the mulberry tree, because he is afraid of having affection for it."

117. *A Wooden Inkstone*

I ask, what do you think
of our beloved northern seaside?
A wooden inkstone of Qin whose grain glitters;
thunder and clouds are hidden in the jagged rock valley.
The elaborate carving is as exquisite as a Go board.
Who made it? Kongsuban.[277]
This artifact handed down for two hundred years in the Ch'a family
is intact, because they cherished it.
Sŏngnyu[278] said he can loan but never give it to me.
I cannot explain why.
I keep it in the center of my room, along with a Hŭgsimha stone inkstone.[279]
Children fear its ragged python-like shape.

---

[277] 公輸般 Gongshu Pan: A legendary Lu dynasty carpenter, who was said to have carved a wooden kite, which did not fall from the sky for three days.
[278] The name of Ch'a Yaksu, son of Ikam, Ch'a Ijin's brother. See #71.
[279] About this inkstone, see #40.

THINKING WINDOW VERSES

118. *Otter Fur Mosŏn*[280]

I ask, what do you think
of our beloved northern seaside?
Made from cloud-patterned silk with otter-fur-wrapped
  handles,
it was good enough to protect your face in a winter storm.
Chŏng Hŭngsin of Paeksangpo bought it last winter
from a horse dealer in Simgyŏng.[281]
Taking pity on an exile with cold, chapped hands,
he sent me this precious thing to spare me more illness—
one p'ok[282] of jade-colored mermaid-woven silk
edged with blue fur thick as a palm.
It was too precious for a poor scholar to keep.
What does it matter if someone stole it?

Paeksangbo is a placename in Kilju. Chŏng Hŭngsin's other name is Yangjung. I grew close to this rich merchant in Yŏngbuk.

---

[280] A winter muffler used by high governmental officials, with two fur handles attached to a folded square of silk.
[281] 瀋京 Fanjing: One of the capitals of the Late Jin dynasty.
[282] A p'ok is 110 cm.

119. *A Marten Hwiyang*[283]

I ask, what do you think
of our beloved northern seaside?
A round marten *hwiyang* on which 卍 is carved—
Yi Chungbae[284] bought it at a pier in Hach'e
and sent it to me along with a letter
when my servant Wi returned from the port of Sŏra last fall.
Impossible not to accept it; also disrespectful.
My friend's affection is beautiful!
I had a similar one in Seoul made of flattened giant timber bamboo—
Wi says it has a different use, since it cannot keep me warm.
Now it's so cold my ears are frozen.
How can I survive the dying year in this short cotton piece?

Hach'e is a place in Myŏngch'ŏn flush with rich businessmen and merchants.

---

[283] A winter cap for men in the Chosŏn period, with an open top and a long back; the smaller ones covered the back of the head and neck, the longer ones, the shoulder and back, and the muff, the cheeks and nape. The nobility favored marten fur while the poor preferred weasel.
[284] See # 70. Yi Chungbae's other name was Taesuk; he was a military official under An Ch'aek, Kim Ryŏ's cousin.

THINKING WINDOW VERSES

120. *At the Grave of Lady Uman*

I ask, what do you think
of our beloved northern seaside?
Magpies cry over the stones heaped at the edge of the
  pond.
Lady Uman[285] is buried in this valley.
Ten million wild pear trees grow here,
and in spring their flowers are in full bloom.
Before the grave lies a stone table one cha high;
a hollow stone cup stands obliquely on it.
Once, drunk, I lay down on the table and saw
in a dream a heavenly angel open the throne.
A ray of red candlelight shone from the sky
and two rows of jade-colored, fragrant ladies passed me by.

The pond is located ten li north of the town. Uman is the name of the valley. I wrote Writings about Godly Things in Uman *separately.*

---

[285] A daughter of the Barbarian King in Kim Ryŏ's *Passing the Grave of Lady Uman.*

121. *Dying Postal Horses*

I ask, what do you think
of our beloved northern seaside?
Dead postal horses were piled up daily
last year at the Sŏkpo station in Puryŏng.
According to one baseless rumor, Lord Charyu[286] was angered
by the people's poor service to the Majo god.[287]
I said, "That can't be true.
Majo has no reason to hate Chang Se'o."
The station manager asked me to write a funeral address
for the horses, petitioning Majo:
"Please resuscitate the dead horses, make them good and fat,
expel contagious diseases, rid us of this vicious energy."

The station is northeast of the fortress. People call the god of horses, "Lord Charyu." All five horses belonging to Chang Se'o, the station manager, died this year of a contagious disease.

---

[286] Charyu was originally a red horse with a black mane. The word refers to good horses. Lord is an honorific title given to things like houses, lands, trees, and stones in shaman rituals.
[287] The patron god of horses. There was an altar to the Majo god outside Tongdaemun Gate in the Chosŏn period.

122. Frequent Eclipses

I ask, what do you think
of our beloved northern seaside?
There was a total eclipse of the sun in October 1798,
and another one the next autumn, which twisted longitude
    and latitude.
Stars lost their place, and noon turned dark
on the first day of the leap month in 1800.[288]
Ice covered trees, there was an earthquake,
and I, deserted, cried alone in my room.
Farmers ran away to hide, and women sighed,
but the district magistrate threw a party and enjoyed
    himself.
They don't care if the sky falls and the earth shakes.
This treacherous party is truly wicked.

When a solar eclipse occurred in 1799, Yu Sangnyang, the regional military commander, did not order a drum to be beaten or a ritual to be performed to stop the eclipse,[289] choosing instead to throw a large drinking party in the Sŭnghwaru Pavilion.

---

[288] This phrase seems to refer to the death of King Chŏngjo.
[289] When a solar or lunar eclipse occurred in the Chosŏn dynasty, the king performed a ritual in the palace courtyard. He and his cabinet wore mourning clothes and prayed until the sun and moon regained their shapes. The morning assembly was suspended, music was forbidden, and the hanging of sinners and slaughter of animals were banned. The local government performed a similar ritual. The magistrate wore mourning clothes with black leg belts, seated in the middle of the yard, and ordered a blind man to beat the drum until the moon and sun regained their shapes.

KIM RYŎ

123. A Special Army Envoy's Behavior: Bootlicking the Powerful

I ask, what do you think
of our beloved northern seaside?
The sins of the chief border inspectors weighed more than
 ten thousand deaths;
people spoke of the renowned Yi family and descendants
 of Yun—
their power, the fuss they made over everything,
the "King's secret orders" always coming from the palace.
Licking their bums and sores was not enough—
they acted cute for them, like a kneeling maid or groveling
 man servant.
All twenty-four towns south of Sŏnch'ullyŏng Pass
and north of Ch'ŏllyŏng held their breath.
How can I become a chief persecutor like Koyo[290]
to root out those who covet wealth and fame, and punish
 them?

Sŏnch'ullyŏng Pass is north of the Tuman River, where Lord Munsuk Yun Kwan[291] drew the boundary and struggled to keep order. Presently, it is part of the Yŏnggot'ap area.

---

[290] 皋陶 Gaotao: A statesman in the court of Emperor Shun who, as the official in charge of persecution and punishment, established the Five Punishments, a series of physical penalties that included tattooing, amputation, castration, and death.
[291] A military general during the reign of Yejong in the Koryŏ dynasty, who led 1,700 soldiers in 1197 to drive the Jurchen people out of the northeast and then built nine fortresses.

124. *Yŏnhŭi's House Red with Maple Leaves*

I ask, what do you think
of our beloved northern seaside?
High was the autumn sky, confederate roses fell like white dew,
and the maples in Yŏnhŭi's yard turned dark red.
Ten thousand leaves lit the crimson sky,
iridescent when the silk drapes were drawn.
Yŏnhŭi met the moon under the dark red trees,
plucking the lonely geomungo in the moonlight.
I was crossing the cold river at the time.
We sat among the leaves in the yard and had a friendly chat.
When we were done, I held her hand
and loitered in the yard red with maple leaves.

There was a maple forest in Yŏnhŭi's yard, adjacent to the San'gosujangnu Pavilion. When autumn comes, it turns a beautiful shade of dark red.

125. *Strong Northern Youths*

I ask, what do you think
of our beloved northern seaside?
What's the best place to entertain in this town?
The magistrate's office, where willow trees droop over the
 Sŏkkyo Bridge.
Strong northern youths with silk bands wrapped around
 their heads
gather here in late spring to play soccer,
run like the wind, enjoy ssirŭm.[292]
No one can match them in the eleven towns north of
 Mach'ŏllyŏng Pass.
The Tŏkwŏn and Tŏkhae brothers are surely the best of
 all.
They slay tigers, they are dead shots.
Truly, they are equal to Chillong.[293]

Tŏkwŏn's other name is Wŏnbo. Tŏkhae's older brother, he was the Chehal[294] of the Pu.

---

[292] Korean wrestling.
[293] 秦隴 Qin Long: Refers to Qinling 秦嶺 and Zhangshan 隴山, rugged towns in Shanxisheng.
[294] A military official in charge of keeping public security.

THINKING WINDOW VERSES

126. *Brave Chehal Yi*

I ask, what do you think
of our beloved northern seaside?
Who is the best among the old veterans of Puryŏng?
Chehal Yi is the strongest of all.
He is quick and energetic even in his seventies.
Drawing an arrow with a stone arrowhead on a four-cha
   horn bow,
he clutches a whip in one hand, leaps onto his horse,
and gallops like a bird in flight.
He recently taught his grandson how to read
and sometimes casts a fishing line into the clear creek.
Man forgets fish, fish forgets water;
this old man lives life as he will.

Chehal's name is Chaeuk; his other name is Ukchi; and his grandson Ŭikyŏm's other name is Peakhwa. I taught him some texts, and he showed some literary promise.

KIM RYŎ

127. *Careless Old Man Nam*

I ask, what do you think
of our beloved northern seaside?
Old man Nam, my neighbor to the west, is carefree.
A clear creek flows east and north of his house.
His oldest son drives an ox, his second son pulls a wagon,
his grandson catches fish, his daughter-in-law weaves cloth.
He drinks a bowl of makgeolli every day
and guards his crops from crows, coming and going in his
    fields.
I have lived through life's vicissitudes
and realize that a learned man is liable to suffer disaster.
I wish I had a ploughshare with a big wooden handle
so that I could grow old, farming like him.

The old man's name is Chesong. His sons, Sŏngkŭk and Sŏngsam, are hard-working farmers who lead prosperous lives. Sŏngkŭk is also a fine equestrian and archer.

THINKING WINDOW VERSES

128. *The Three Brother of Pujang[295] Chŏng*

I ask, what do you think
of our beloved northern seaside?
The three brothers of Pujang Chŏng were wise and skilled,
competing neck and neck with one another.
They were masters of the eighteen martial arts
and good at almost everything.
They played geomungo and pipe well,
and they could easily embroider two horses in a day.
Heaven gave birth to Langja, who couldn't find a spouse;
they were like Yŏnsoŭl.[296]
They brought every color of thread—red, blue, yellow, and black—
and bound books by the clear window for me.

The three brothers Chŏng, Wŏnsu, Wŏnjik, and Wŏnhŭng, were all good with their hands.

---

[295] A military official.
[296] 燕小乙 Yanxiaoyi: nicknames for Yanqing; also called 浪子 Langzi. A clever character in *Shui Hu Zhuan* [水滸傳 *Water Margin*], he excelled in both literary and martial arts.

129. *A Chaste Woman, Mrs. Wu*

I ask, what do you think
of our beloved northern seaside?
Brave chaste Mrs. Wu of Satongjin!
Such a spirit, shining like the sun and stars, is hard to find
  in any age.
When a thief broke into her house, her mother-in-law ran
  away,
but she confronted him alone with her bare hands.
Stabbed eight times in the face, she grabbed
a wooden pole to hold herself up and called him "a pig and
  a dog."
I heard the police chief was bribed to bury the case.
Toho, Toho, son of a noble family, how can you
still rule the town, ignorant of ethics?

Satongjin is on the east side of town. A man called Nam Sangbok from Sanwŏn tried to rape Mrs. Wu and ended up killing her. The police chief, Ch'oe Ch'angsi, suppressed news of the crime. I wrote The Life of Wua *separately.*

THINKING WINDOW VERSES

130. *Judas Tree*

I ask, what do you think
of our beloved northern seaside?
Judas trees[297] circle the stone steps around the water deer's
    eye-like fence[298]
and stretch their branches over the garden filled with pink
    blossoms.
Fragrant buds grow on every calyx from the same root
and tens of thousands of flowers open.
When the wind blows, pink flowers flutter like snow,
and when a wagtail alights on one, the shadow of its bough
    trembles.
An older brother is separated from his younger and vice
    versa;
they miss each other, weeping at the edge of the sky.
Layers of deep water and craggy hills stand in the way
of what I anxiously gaze toward, my eyes growing dimmer.

The northern fence around Yŏnhŭi's house is covered with Judas trees.

---

[297] The judas tree is a symbol of brotherly love. Kim Ryŏ's younger brother, Kim Sŏn, was implicated in Kang Ich'ŏn's obscenity case and exiled to Ch'osan in Pyŏngan Province.
[298] A diamond-shaped fence, which resembles the eyes of a water deer.

131. *The Day the Snow Covered the Whole Earth*

I ask, what do you think
of our beloved northern seaside?
The north wind howled, and a cold rain fell.
When the rain stopped, snow covered the whole earth.
Snow fell like balls of cotton, flattening in the street,
and blew through the window, like sprinkled salt.
In a moment, thousands of houses were buried in snow.
I closed the gate and windows, then lit the blue oil lamp.
A drifter from the south couldn't bear the cold
and clicked his tongue in lamentation, ceaselessly weeping.
How grateful I was for Togam[299] Chang of the eastern village,
who broke through the snowstorm with wine to console me.

Togam Chang's name was Unik; his other name was Saryong. He was Chang Ilwhan's uncle and Kim Hoeik's maternal grandfather.

---

[299] The title of a petty provincial official.

132. *Daylilies*

I ask, what do you think
of our beloved northern seaside?
Desolate autumn rain falls on dry boughs
and drips from the daylilies under the stone steps.
Because they have long been known as the "anxiety-
 forgetting plant,"
I transplanted several stems from a green mountain slope.
How could I know I would fret more, not less,
even after toiling to heap dirt on them?
The things of the world go up and down—it is the way of
 nature.
Foolish is the man who favors old customs in a frivolous
 time.
Call him "an anxiety plant" from now on.
It would be better to throw him away in the street.

133. The Married Buddhist Monk of the Namsŏksa Temple

I ask, what do you think
of our beloved northern seaside?
The monk of the Namsŏk Temple harvested millet
to make wine to sell and then marry off his daughter.
The wedding guests of monks and laymen mixed,
vying to devour steamed dog meat and pork.
The couple's names were written on yellow marriage letter paper.
Where was this kept? In a red box, of course.
His face had a rash,[300] his head was shaved smooth,
he recited "Namuamit'abul"[301] in a loud voice.
Saints reformed this world into a civilized society,
but how can such a man still exist?

Namsŏksa was the name of a Buddhist temple. Monks in Kwanbuk had wives and children and were thus called "Married Buddhist

---

[300] A character in *Yangju Pyŏlsandae Nori* (Mask Dance) and *Songp'a Sandae Nori* (Mask Dance), this monk entered the secular world to act dishonorably and was infected with scabies.

[301] The most common Buddhist chant, which means, "Save us, merciful Buddha." Here the Buddha is Amitabha Buddha, the central Buddha of Pure Land Buddhism.

THINKING WINDOW VERSES

Priests."[302] *Mr. Sŏ, the owner of my rented house, married his son to a monk's daughter.*

---

[302] In the villages of Puryŏng, Kyŏnghŭng, Hoeryŏng, Ŭnsŏng, and Chongsŏng, Buddhist monks worked together to build a community temple. According to one authority, when Yunkwan drove the Jurchens out and built nine castles, he let them continue to live there. They were called Married Buddhist monks because they shaved their heads.

134. Fishermen North of the Northern Mach'ŏllyŏng Pass[303]

I ask, what do you think
of our beloved northern seaside?
Fishermen in the four towns north of Mach'ŏllyŏng Pass
 sold their boats and scattered.
The new king ordered a reduction in the amount of fish
 offered to him,
but provincial officials, feigning ignorance, exploited them
 more.
Last year the Injŏngga[304] was thirty strings of coins;
this year it soared above two hundred.
It's hard to live, even if you must sell your wife and children,
but provincial officials rob them again.
Besides, bad weather ruins fishing.
Better to run away as soon as you can.

The four towns of Myŏngch'ŏn, Kilju, Kyŏngsŏng, and Puryŏng offer fish to the king. Last winter, he halted these winter offerings, but Governor Yi Pyŏngjŏng did not return them to the fishermen, saying he had already given them to the king.

---

[303] A pass between Tanch'ŏn-gun, South Hamgyŏng Province and Haksŏng-gun, North Hamgyŏng Province, south of the Mach'ŏllyŏng Mountains, seven hundred meters above sea level.
[304] Refers to the additional money or things (mainly rice, which was called Injŏng rice) that petty officials demanded from the people when they paid their taxes.

135. *Water Mills*

I ask, what do you think
of our beloved northern seaside?
There are many bends in the creeks of Puryŏng,
and rows of water mills stand in those bends.
When the creeks rise as spring gives way to summer,
the roaring sounds of water and milling compete.
The anxious exile cannot sleep,
his heart aching all night long from the noise.
The mill has saved manpower since time immemorial;
it doesn't cost much to install it.
I wish billions of stone mortars were made
and distributed to every creek in southern towns.

136. *Melon Farming*

I ask, what do you think
of our beloved northern seaside?
The people of Puryŏng were so poor
they planted melons on the western slope of the castle gate.
When the melons ripened to cover the roadside fields,
they sold them to buy grain to mill.
Last year, most of the melons withered on the vine.
Mr. Kim and Mr. Chang suffered the most.
Everyone told me, "You don't have to worry, sir,
because your servant is like an ox and your horse is strong."
I laughed out loud. What difference is there
in the politics of No and Wi?[305]

Kim Yunt'ae of Sunch'ŏn Pu and Chang Munje of Kosŏng-gun were poor migrants who sold melons.

---

[305] From *The Analects of Confucius*, Book XIII: "The governments of the states of Lu and Wei are like older and younger brothers."

137. *Karich'on Hot Springs*

I ask, what do you think
of our beloved northern seaside?
It was warm and bright in mid-February.
Yŏnhŭi's letter stirred me from my drowsiness.
I opened it to find nothing special:
"The western part of town is called Karich'on;
the hot springs lie ten li away from there.
The upper spring isn't hot, but the middle one is.
The fir tree in front of the spring is a thousand kil[306] high and green.
The broad rock beside the tree is flat as a cushion.
I will sit there and dry my hair.
When you come, look for the rock."

There are dozens of houses at the entrance to the valley. The hot spring is in T'anggol.

---

[306] Traditional Korean measure, usually referring to someone's height, about 2.4-3 m.

138. *Drinking Companions in Puryŏng*

I ask, what do you think
of our beloved northern seaside?
We were eight drinking companions in Puryŏng,
including Paengnŭng and me, all of us old.
Eldery Chang drank like an ox and couldn't keep his balance.
Ikpo could drink a hundred cups a day.
Tamsu preferred rice-wine filtered cake to steamed rice.
Mr Kwŏn's son grew meek when dead drunk.
Munji's eyes were glued to the wine jars,
and Ŏnso drank directly from the jug.
I'm sad because we cannot meet. I miss you all.
My aching heart is almost breaking.

Ikpo is Old Chang Kukpo's cousin; his other name is Munch'ik. Munsŏng is Tamsu's cousin; his other name is Munji. Chang Ŏnso's other name is Sŏnsul. All are clerks in the barracks.

THINKING WINDOW VERSES

139. *The Price of Salt Skyrocketed*

I ask, what do you think
of our beloved northern seaside?
Iron salt is better than earth salt north of Mach'ŏllyŏng Pass;
it's finer, softer, white, tastes good.
When it's cheap, three mal[307] of salt equal one mal of rice.
But when there's a shortage, it costs the same as rice.
Lately the price of salt has skyrocketed,
and you can't get one mal of salt even for five mal of rice.
Old people in the north cry,
"The sight of a dining table makes us nauseous. How can we eat any food?
We haven't had salt for six months, thanks to the virtue
of the governor who was appointed this year!"[308]

When the new governor, Yi Pyŏngjŏng, raised the salt tax too much, most salt producers fled. Two doe[309] of salt were equal to one mal of rice for the public.

---

[307] A traditional Korean unit of measuring grain and liquor, equivalent to eighteen liters.

[308] On 20 August 1800, *The Chronicles of Sunjo* reported that "He appointed Yi Pyŏngjŏng as the governor of Hamgyŏng Province."

[309] A traditional Korean unit of measuring grain and liquor, equivalent to 1.8 liters.

140. *Kidnapped Miss Kwak*

I ask, what do you think
of our beloved northern seaside?
Miss Kwak was living in Tonggok
when a young man kidnapped her in the middle of the night.
Tightly bound, she couldn't shout,
and her parents stamped their feet hard enough to overturn the sky.
It was said the young man was a petty official in town,
a marriage pillager in collusion with the district office.
There were some strange customs in the north.
Last winter, Pukp'yŏngsa[310] sent an official order,
which the district governments did not distribute, and the people ignored.
Only those who heard about it got their backs up in vain.

Ma Ŏnbang was a petty official, whose sister, Kyesŏm, was a favorite of Yu Sangnyang. Ma Ŏnbang raped Miss. Kwak. Because forced marriage was common in the north, my elder brother An issued a special document prohibiting it.

---

[310] The sixth-ranked military official in charge of general management.

THINKING WINDOW VERSES

141. *A True Scholar, Mr. Hong*

I ask, what do you think
of our beloved northern seaside?
Poor Mr. Hong of Sunam had terrible luck,
supporting his elderly parents and reading books even while plowing.
In the morning, he drove his ox to the green field by the slope,
bound his book to its horns, and read aloud.
When he was done plowing, he was tired,
and sweat streamed down him like rain, but he kept reading.
I dare say Mr. Hong is a very strange scholar,
like Tong, Anp'ung's[311] filial son.
I'm sorry not to have Ch'angryŏ's[312] skill at writing.
How can I write a long poem praising Hong?

Sunam is a placename. There are two villages in Ch'ŏngam, Sunam and Subuk. Hong's other name is Sŏngsa.

---

[311] Kim Ryŏ is mistaken: Anfeng's filial son was Lixing, not Dong. The filial son Dong was Dongyong of the Late Han dynasty.
[312] 昌黎 Chānglí: Refers to Han Yu, a great Tang dynasty writer. Chānglí was his penname.

142. *A Confusing World of Requests and Disputes*

I ask, what do you think
of our beloved northern seaside?
Who is the best calligrapher among Puryŏng's petty officials?
People say Pak Kyŏngsil ranks first and Kwŏn Ch'ungguk second.
They know how to select a good horse, but they can only see what it looks like.
How can they judge the sturdiness of its frame with their eyes?
Petty official Ch'oe was finally recognized as a leader.
It was only natural that the Jin dynasty weakened as the Chu grew stronger.
The muddle and purity of worldly things are mixed up:
an uncut gem from Jing Mountain [313] is priceless, but mubu[314] is more valued.
What son of any family will enter government service?
There were Nanyangwi[315] even in peaceful times.

The petty official's name was Ch'oe Tohyŏng; he was Paekgnŭng's maternal uncle, celebrated for his calligraphy. But there was only some artistry in his brushstrokes.

---

[313] Generally regarded as the most precious thing in the world.
[314] A gem with a white pattern on a red surface, which resembles jade.
[315] 爛羊胃 Lanyangwei: A metaphor for an unqualified government official.

THINKING WINDOW VERSES

143. *I Met Sir Ian in My Dream*

I ask, what do you think
of our beloved northern seaside?
I remember lying against the bookcase one night last fall
when Sir Ian came to see me. We greeted each other cordially,
and when I approached him with short, quick steps, bowing politely,
he remained silent, as if troubled.
I sat beside him and lowered my head,
tears welling as from a clear spring.
At once he stood up, solemnly,
and I followed him to the swamp—
which was too rough and steep to cross.
When I woke, the waning moon was moving toward dawn.

Lord Ch'oe Ianjae's name was Pyŏngok; his other name was Kun'gyŏng. He was a friend of my father.

144. *The Reclusive Scholar Yi of Yongsŏng*

I ask, what do you think
of our beloved northern seaside?
The reclusive scholar Yi of Yongsŏng[316]
hid his talent for half his life, but his name was known.
Because he read ten thousand books,
the royal court invited the wise man to work there.
But Yi adamantly refused to take a government position,
and mugwort grew thick on his shut twig gate.
He constantly waved off Mr. Ch'ae and Mr. Chu,
which is possible only for those who transcend the secular world.
Last winter, he sent another letter to old man Ch'a,
who illuminated the honorable eternal truth, thanks to him.

The reclusive scholar was Yi Wŏnbae.[317] Ch'ae Hongdŭk and Chu Kwanggyŏm of Chongsŏng studied under Ch'ae Chegong. His letter to Ch'a Namkyu is included in Hwat'angsŏn'ŏ.

---

[316] Another name for Kyŏngsŏng in Hamgyŏng Province.
[317] 李元培 (1745-1802): A scholar in the middle Chosŏn period. His other name was Yŏdal; his penname was Kuam. Learned in classics and renowned for his scholarship, he wrote *The Collected Works of Kuam*. When King Chŏngjo recruited obscure scholars, Hamgyŏng Province recommended him to the royal court, where he answered the sixty questions about the classics and received an award. But poor health prevented him from entering government service. He was appointed an educational official of Hamgyŏng Province.

THINKING WINDOW VERSES

145. *Local Produce in Puryŏng*

I ask, what do you think
of our beloved northern seaside?
I used to hear only bad things about Puryŏng,
but now the thought of it gladdens my heart.
Rice grains are oily, millet is fragrant,
the delicacies of the land are rich, the seafood is excellent.
The brackens in T'anggol valley are fat as fists,
and sea bream in the southern port are as big as flying fish.
Cold, sweet water in the well is clear and deep,
and the climate is cool and bright.
Now I fill my stomach with baked crab.
Sea, not sky, is what I see here in the south.

The ports of Namban and Tongban lie sixty li east of town, where sea bream as large as a portable dining table are caught.

146. *Where I Wander Even in Dream*

I ask, what do you think
of our beloved northern seaside?
One year has already passed since I was driven to the south.
Green leaves turned yellow and fell.
Tears fall when I raise and lower my head,
dappling my shabby sleeves.
My soul wanders even in dream
south of Sŏkpo and west of Ch'ŏnggye.
However nice this may be, it's not my home,
and I can't understand why I miss it so much.
When it's impossible for me to return to my hometown,
how can I go back to that blue seaside?

THINKING WINDOW VERSES

147. *The First Full Moon of the Year*

I ask, what do you think
of our beloved northern seaside?
I still remember a huge crowd of people in town competing
to be the first to see the moon on the night of Taeborŭm.[318]
Where to go, I wondered, taking my cane.
The sun set on the Ch'ŏnyŏngnu Pavilion,
where it was quiet, with fine screens drawn around.
Inside was a beauty named Yŏnhŭi,
with a pomegranate-colored scarlet skirt embroidered with butterflies
and an apricot-colored jacket speckled with mandarin ducks.
To ensure she would bear a son, she waited quietly
under the hardy rubber tree to be the first to see the moon rise.[319]

---

[318] The day of the first full moon of the year.
[319] There is a folk belief that the first person to see the moon rise on Taeborŭm will bear a son.

KIM RYŎ

148. Despicable Toho Yu[320]

I ask, what do you think
of our beloved northern seaside?
What a despicable man—Toho Yu!
What resentment did he harbor to torture people so?
When they were deep in mourning,[321]
how could he keep catching and stoning them?
Evil officials continued to trap and shackle people,
stomping on them atop shards of glass, abusing them to death.
Because heaven was originally just and fair,
the conspiracy of Hwangyang[322] failed.
I cannot say everything; my pounding heart shudders—
I am still startled in my dreams.

Hwangyang—1799—refers to the imprisonment of Kim Chongwŏn and Chang Se'o.

---

[320] Refers to the local military commander, Yu Sangnyang.
[321] A period of national mourning after King Chŏngjo's death.
[322] 1799, the twenty-third year of King Chŏngjo's reign.

149. Grave of Skeletons

I ask, what do you think
of our beloved northern seaside?
In a secluded spot ten li from the western gate of Puryŏng
   Fortress,
white skeletons were heaped from the past.
When the Japanese invaded and war broke out,
ten thousand volunteer soldiers died in a single day.
The general beat his breast, crying bitterly.
Red grudge-stained blood overflowed the valley.
People politely gathered the remains, obeying the king's
   order,
and buried a mountain of skeletons in one place.
Green moss covers earthly flowers, death fire rises,
and when rain falls, the sound of sobbing fills the valley.

There is a large mound ten li from the western gate, where the military commander Wŏn Hwi[323] fought to his death during the Japanese invasion of 1592. I wrote The Beginning and the End of Wŏn Hwi's Death in the War *separately.*

---

[323] Wŏn Hwi (1543 – 1592). His other name was Pakwi. He won first prize in the military official examination in 1576; as the Puryŏng military commander he recruited volunteer soldiers during the Japanese invasion of 1592 and died fighting at Immyŏng, Kilju.

KIM RYŎ

150. *Mrs. Yun, a Virtuous Woman Who Killed a Tiger*

I ask, what do you think
of our beloved northern seaside?
I pay my respects at the red gate of the virtuous woman,
    Mrs. Yun,
where the pond lies in blue mist and the green willow
    flutters.
When her husband went into the mountains to gather
    wood
a tiger attacked him with its bared teeth.
Infuriated, she raised her pretty arms
to beat the tiger with all her might.
When she had used up her strength, the tiger died.
Her husband pulled himself out of its mouth and ran to
    the pond.
Even now, the place where that virtuous woman beat the
    tiger to death
is covered with grotesque rocks and thick forests.

Five li south of town is the red gate of Mrs. Yun, wife of the scholar, Wŏn Munhoe. This story is recorded in The Story of Loyal and True Women of Puryŏng Fortress.

THINKING WINDOW VERSES

151. *Lord Sŏ Chisu's[324] Wise Ruling*

I ask, what do you think
of our beloved northern seaside?
The old men of Puryŏng laughed out loud,
claiming that Lord Sŏ Munch'ŏng is truly a living Buddha.
"He loved people like his own children, and he was
so sweet and affectionate that a mottled pheasant sang in his office.[325]
Our commoners have lived peacefully for sixty years,
thanks to Lord Munch'ŏng's benevolence.
Our bodies are old, our hair is grey, and we don't like
to think about changes in the world, because nothing goes right.
Lord Han and Lord Yu have a different disposition:
they bring calamity and harm to the people."

Premier Sŏ Chisu was a wise ruler of this town. He even tamed creatures, like the pheasant that nested on the steppingstones. Han Ŭnggŏm and Yu Sangnyang were greedy officials.

---

[324] Sŏ Chisu (1714~1768): A statesman in the late Chosŏn period. His other name was Ilji, his penname was Song'ong, and he was a premier. Munch'ŏng is his posthumous epithet.

[325] This is a widely quoted anecdote about good governance. When 魯恭 Lu Gong in the Late Han dynasty ruled wisely as a governor of 中牟縣 Zhongmu County, three mysterious things happened. The rice borer rampant in a neighboring town did not invade his town, a pheasant trained by Lu Gong stayed by his side, and good-hearted children did not catch the pheasant, which bore chicks. 後漢書 卷25 魯恭傳

152. Mrs. Ch'oe,[326] a Virtuous Woman

I ask, what do you think
of our beloved northern seaside?
Virtuous Mrs. Kang came from the Ch'oe family,
she was chaste and strong-willed.
No one was there when she killed herself at midnight,
an auspicious bolt of purple lightening flashing in the eaves.
Inbo[327] wrote a long ode to Tobo,[328]
but I pity my poor writing, a dog tail before a marten's.
Her husband was Tŏkso's father
and a brother of Ŭng'ya's grandfather.
From ancient times, many talented men have descended
   from famous families.
Someday they will hold up the sky with their two hands.

Mrs. Ch'oe was Kang Suse's wife, Ŭng'ya's great grandfather. I wrote "Epitaph of Mrs. Ch'oe" and "Fifty Rhymes for Mrs. Ch'oe, a Virtuous Woman."

---

[326] In Korea, a woman keeps her maiden name even after marriage. That is why the virtuous woman, Mrs. Kang, was called Mrs. Ch'oe.
[327] Yi Yŏngik's other name, a literary man and calligrapher.
[328] Yi Kwangsa's other name, a calligrapher in the late Chosŏn period.

THINKING WINDOW VERSES

153. *Transcendent Sŭng*[329] *Kim*

I ask, what do you think
of our beloved northern seaside?
Sŭng Kim of Subuk showed little emotion,
but since he did what he was supposed to do, even women
   and children liked him.
After drinking ten thousand cups of wine, he would break
   into loud laughter,
and when there was nothing to do in the Pu office, he
   would sing and chant.
He never lost his temper when he was rebuked,
kept his mouth shut, didn't know how to flatter
   P'yŏngjinhu.[330]
When everyone got drunk, he got drunk—
he didn't care about the mud, drinking the dregs.
Sŭng Kim was indeed a transcendent man—
a Paeksi[331]-like person we can ask for help with any
   problem.

Sŭng Kim's name was Ihwa; his other name was Ŭikyŏng. His ancestor Chŏn was a martyr in the Japanese invasion of 1592. He

---

[329] A petty official in the local government.
[330] 平津侯 Pingjinhou: Refers to Gongsuhong, a scholar in the Han dynasty. When he became a minister, he built a guest house with a small door facing east for receiving people.
[331] 伯始 Bóshǐ: Huguang's other name in the late Han dynasty. He was so learned that people would visit him even at the age of eighty seeking solutions for controversies at the royal court.

showed little emotion from his youth, but he was on bad terms with Sŭng Pak Hongjung[332] and formed a separatist group.

---

[332] About Sŭng Pak Hongjung. See # 18.

154. *Yu Kyŏngbu, My Student*

I ask, what do you think
of our beloved northern seaside?
The customs of the Musan and Mohe people[333] are similar,
but Kyŏngbu is quite extraordinary.
He was one of my first students here,
fearless as Chungyu of Wi.[334]
Last winter, when a blizzard filled the sky
and cattle couldn't move more than a few paces,
he braved the snow to visit me,
lugging a jar of wine and fatty meat on his shoulder.
He didn't seem to mind his chapped hands and cheeks flushed with cold.
I don't know how to repay his generosity in such dire circumstances.

Confucian student T'aengno's other name is Kyŏngbu. His father Sŏnghun was a clerk in Musan.

---

[333] The Mohe or Malgal 靺鞨 were a Tungusic people in ancient Manchuria.
[334] 仲由 Zhong You: One of Confucius's most renowned and faithful disciples, commonly known as Zilu. Confucius said that "Zilu is braver than me."

KIM RYŎ

155. *Memory of Hanging Out with My Students*

I ask, what do you think
of our beloved northern seaside?
Last fall I hung out with my students in Tongjach'e,
but none of them are with me now.
Konso had a cane, Hŭiik stood in the back,
and Kang Sangguk stayed in the middle.
Han'gi, Wŏllyang, and Paekhwa ran on the rugged mountain
like squirrels among rocks, their pigtails swinging.
I recited poems in a soft voice, whistling
and sauntering to a place where autumn leaves gathered and a stream flowed.
How can I enjoy such pleasure in this situation?
The damp poisonous air in the bluish twilight is like a wildfire.

Tongjach'e is located twenty li south of town. Wŏllyang's family name is Pak; his name is Insŏp.

156. *Full Moon in June*

I ask, what do you think
of our beloved northern seaside?
On the night of Yudu,[335] when the full moon rose,
Yŏnhŭi washed her hair in Okp'oktong,
surrounded by blue cliffs like folding screens
and waterfalls lined up like a row of ten thousand jars.
The clean water was numbingly cold in the depths
and clouds lingered, with a tinge of a blue aura.
When I took off my chŏksam to wade in,
Yŏnhŭi cupped water in her hands and spilled it over my back.
She sat modestly on a rock by the water,
her dark eyebrows reflected in the watery moonlight.

---

[335] The day of the full moon in June, a traditional Korean holiday, when people wash their hair in a stream flowing east.

KIM RYŎ

157. *The Vest Noh Simhong Made for Me*

I ask, what do you think
of our beloved northern seaside?
This silk vest Noh made with stringing beads while dozing
   off.
Her skill is comparable to the Vega.
She made a knot, attached minica rings to the moire cloth,
and stitched the edge with lemon yellow silk.
She tied a tongsim knot[336] where the front flaps met,
which means I should cherish her affection like a mountain.
The song of the geese sounds sad among the thick green
   leaves,
the north wind blows like a storm, and the autumn sky is
   far away.
How can I survive without clothes, even arrowroot ones?
I pull on my short cotton cloth, which doesn't cover my
   shins.

Simhong made a vest for me. I wrote A Song for Noh Simghong for Sending Me an Un'gŭmdan Silk Vest.

---

[336] A traditional knot.

THINKING WINDOW VERSES

158. *The Call of Cicadas at the Sŏjangdae Pavilion*

I ask, what do you think
of our beloved northern seaside?
Cicadas fill tens of thousands of trees with song
one summer evening in front of the Sŏjangdae Pavilion.
They swallow wind, drink dew, want nothing.
They shine brightly with lovely wings.
You are Yuhahye,[337] a true noble among noblemen,
who sought concord with others—though he didn't swim
    with the tide.
Your call rings out on the green mountain at twilight;
your clear, clean music goes everywhere.
I plan to write a dancing song with your sound.
How can you partner with lewd peeping frogs and narrow-
    mouthed toads?

The pavilion is outside the western gate, in a thick forest. Cicadas sing loudly in summer.

---

[337] 柳下惠 Liuxia Hui: A statesman and thinker in the Liu dynasty. Mencius praised him as "a man who devoted himself to making concord with others."

159. *A Sparrow Hawk*

I ask, what do you think
of our beloved northern seaside?
I bought a sparrow hawk from a Manchurian merchant.
It had white hair and shining golden eyes,
it was small, skilled, swift, and wild as a peregrine falcon.
I left it in Kyeham's[338] care,
planning to go hawking with him in the fall.
But Commander Toho, urged on by the provincial office,
was said to monitor and torment my students.
I was close to Kyeham, and there was no way he would be safe.
The same held for an insignificant creature.

Yi Pyŏngjŏng urged the new Toho Commander Yi Kaphoe to arrest sixty of my students. They were interrogated and tormented. I don't know what became of them.

---

[338] The other name of Chi Tŏkhae. See #54.

160. *After Leaving Yŏnhŭi*

I ask, what do you think
of our beloved northern seaside?
When I parted from Yuninja[339] last year,
the pain nearly killed me, as if my eyes were pierced and
 my bowels sliced open.
This year, when I parted from Yŏnhŭi,
it was just like parting from Yuninja.
Finding a true friend is so hard:
What sadness compares to being torn apart?
I used to drink and sing in the Ch'ŏnyŏngnu Pavilion,
promising to live to a hundred, singing in the morning,
 drinking at night.
But the next life is unimaginable, and here is the end of
 this life.
The cloud in Kangdong and the tree in Wisu,[340] separated,
 cry in vain.

---

[339] Kim Chosun's penname. See #39.
[340] Refers to Du Fu's poem, "Thinking of Li Bai on a Spring Day": "A tall tree stands in the spring sky north of Weishui, and a cloud at twilight east of the river."—separated, that is, by a great distance. Du Fu lived in Weishui (渭水), Li Bai in Jiangdong (江東).

161. *The Poems of Pak, a Village School Teacher*

I ask, what do you think
of our beloved northern seaside?
Pak, the village schoolteacher in Ch'ŏnsudong,
read books, as if scratching the top of his foot with his shoes on.
Many poems stored in the dusty box were incomprehensible,
like barbarian music or the language of shrikes.
They were so ridiculous they left me speechless,
they tasted like a watermelon rind.
Pointlessly sad in his eighties,
he tried to learn Tang poems,[341] straying further yet.
Old man, old man, please stop writing.
And don't blame Chigongkŏ.[342]

Ch'ŏnsudong is a place in Musan. The teacher was named Pak Sŏ, and he was Sŭng Pak Hongjung's father-in-law. His grotesque poems were difficult to understand.

---

[341] Tang dynasty poems are regarded as the best of Chinese poetry.
[342] Examiner of the state examination for government officials during the Koryŏ period.

THINKING WINDOW VERSES

162. *A Disabled Person, Chiyŏkyo*

I ask, what do you think
of our beloved northern seaside?
Chiyŏkyo was a disabled man in Murŭng;
his legs were crippled, and he had only one eye.
Yet he was intrepid, a brave spirit,
like a roc bird that flies ten thousand li to the south.[343]
Educated in a village school in his youth,
he easily surpassed his teacher.
Once he visited me at my house in the mountains.
When he held a brush to write poems, they shed brilliant
　　luster.
I held him deep in my heart so as not to forget him.
Now in sadness I gaze at the cold clouds and the dim sun.

Chiyŏkyo's name is Yangnyong.

---

[343] The phrase comes from *Zuangzi*: "When the feng migrates to the Southern Ocean it flaps its wings over the water for 3,000 li. Then it ascends on a whirlwind to 90,000 li, resting only after six months." (*The Writings of Chuang Tzŭ*. Trans. James Legge, 165). That is, he had high aspirations.

163. *Local Officials Who Resemble Toch'ŏl*[344]

I ask, what do you think
of our beloved northern seaside?
It was Turŭng[345] who said in a poem that peacocks have tails
and oxen have horns, and Ak who wrote it down.
Who demanded peacocks' tails and ox horns from the people?
It was calm Lord Yi and furious Lord Yu.[346]
The idiom Chinggangch'wijae[347] is laughable,
too strange and sad to mention again.
After so much suffering, there is little to be happy
or angry about; whether you call it a horse or an ox, I just keep my place.
Whether or not it is a hornless ox has nothing to do with me.
I just can't stand the name Toch'ŏl.

The last military commander, Yi Kwangsŏp, liked peacocks' tails and was thus known as the peacock tail magistrate. Ak was the military clerk Ch'oe Un'ak. This is recorded in Yŏnŭm *Essay.*

---

[344] 饕餮 Taotie: A beast in Chinese legend, which devours its own body; a symbol of lust, which suggests a glutton or a greedy person.
[345] 杜陵 Du Ling: Refers to Du Fu, who wrote "Chixiaoxing," in which he sings of a peacock and a cow.
[346] Refers to Yu Sangnyang.
[347] 懲羹吹齏 cheng geng chui ji: If you burn your mouth with hot soup, eat something cold, like raw fish or vegetables cooled with your breath. The idiom refers to someone who becomes too careful after a setback.

164. *Mr. Hong, Who Killed a Tiger*

I ask, what do you think
of our beloved northern seaside?
Mr. Hong of Kijin came across a tiger at daybreak,
seated with its back to the mountain. When it bared its
    angry teeth,
he didn't even have a scrap of iron in his hand,
so he kicked the blue cliff and rocks cascaded down,
and then he threw a jar-sized rock at the tiger,
breaking its left leg as it rose.
Hong jumped on the tiger, struck it madly, slit its throat.
Heavy sweat like raindrops flowed down his body.
When I met Hong, he was of stout build,
with prominent cheekbones in his dark red face.

Mr. Hong's name was Cheha. He and his older brother Chedŭk were quick and strong. After killing a tiger with his bare hands, he was promoted to Ch'okwan[348] of the town.

---

[348] The ninth-ranked military official in charge of a ch'o, a military unit of one hundred soldiers.

165. *My Beloved Sister*

I ask, what do you think
of our beloved northern seaside?
My sister, my sister, who lives in Seoul—
my heart melts. I haven't seen her for five years.
Young, we clung side by side to our mother,
suckling her breasts together.
When my mother died, I was so lonely
I loved my sister as if she were my mother.
When she sent a letter last year asking after my health,
tears of blood were falling before I had read it halfway
   through.
She sent a white-linen summer cloth to Yŏnhŭi
and a fine cotton yuŭi[349] to me.

---

[349] A man's jacket, which comes down to the hip and has a belt for the waist.

THINKING WINDOW VERSES

166. *Annotating* The Book of Changes

I ask, what do you think
of our beloved northern seaside?
Following in my late father's footsteps with a cane, I examined
the nine teachers'[350] research into *The Book of Changes*.
Yin and yang, strong and weak got mixed up.
After Kyŏngbang[351] and Ch'ogong,[352] phases and lines were confused.
Chŏng Sukja's[353] *Yi Zhuan* followed received opinion,
while Chu Hoeong's[354] *Zhouyi Benyi* investigated too much.
My father asked me in all seriousness to expound on the book;
ten years of annotating it left my hair grey.
Now my position is like Paengno[355] when he lost that note.

---

[350] Nine schools that studied *The Book of Changes* in the Western Han dynasty.

[351] 京房 Jin Fang: A scholar in the Western Han dynasty. He studied divinatory arts under Jian Yanshou, and his prophesies of disasters often occurred.

[352] 焦贛 Jiao Gong: A theorist of divinatory arts in the Western Han dynasty; his other name was Yanshou. He handed down his knowledge to Jin Fang.

[353] 程叔子 Cheng Shuzi: Refers to Cheng Yi, a great scholar in the Song dynasty, called Shuzi to distinguish him from his elder brother, Cheng Hao.

[354] 朱晦翁 Zhu Huiweng: Refers to Zhu Xi, whose penname was Huiweng. He inherited Cheng Zi's teachings and continued to study them.

[355] 伯魯 Bai Lu: Zhao Jianzi had two sons, Bai Lu the elder and Wu Xu the younger. One day he wrote something about discipline and asked them to memorize it. He called them three

I wander on the mountain trails, crying in vain.

I used to keep two books of Zhouyi, *in which my late father made notes. I expounded on the ambiguous passages and edited them into four books titled* An Annotation on The Book of Changes— *which were lost when I was arrested.*

---

years later. The elder son could not recite the note, which he had lost. The younger knew the words by heart. Jianzi dethroned Bai Lu as crown prince and appointed Wu Xu instead.

THINKING WINDOW VERSES

167. *A Contagious Disease*

I ask, what do you think
of our beloved northern seaside?
I still remember the raging epidemic in the spring of 1799,
when the death toll ceaselessly climbed.
I heard that in just two days a hundred thousand bodies
were heaped like a mountain in Seoul.
Five ministers went to Pungmang Mountain[356] one after
    another—
from the beginning the heavenly law must be inhuman.
A dragon ascended into heaven at Chŏngho[357] and never
    returned.
The sun set on Ch'ang'o,[358] adding to my yearning.
Suffering and hardship are inevitable in affairs of the world,
and those who are left behind grieve more than the dead.

Five ministers—Hŏllu Kim, P'yŏngjang Hong Nagsŏng, Kim Hŭi, Ch'aejegong, and Mongsang —passed away within two years.

---

[356] The mountain where the dead are said to go.
[357] According to an old story, when the Emperor made a cauldron by a lake under Jingshan, a dragon came down from the sky. He rode on the dragon, ascending into the sky. Chŏngho thus means the death of a king, in this case the death of King Chŏngjo.
[358] The field where Emperor Shun died.

168. *Chŏng Munbu*[359]

I ask, what do you think
of our beloved northern seaside?
War spread like wildfire in 1592-93,
and people still speak of General Chŏng's feats.
Who said he was a mere scholar stuck at his desk?
He held up the sky with one hand so it would not fall.
Not one out of a million Japanese soldiers survived.
Only wailing sounds of ghosts were heard at Paegt'ap Field.[360]
His service wasn't recognized; instead he was executed.
His poem about King Huai of the Chu dynasty[361] brought

---

[359] (1565~1624): A civil official and general of a volunteer army in the middle Chosŏn period. His penname was Nongp'o; his posthumous title is Ch'ungŭi. The Imjin War broke out in 1592 when he was Commander-in-Chief of the North. When Kuk Kyŏngin and his followers captured Prince Imhae and Prince Sunhwa and handed them over to the Japanese general, Kiyomasa, he was infuriated, organized a volunteer army, and defeated them at Paet'ap Field. Falsely accused of involvement in the Yi Kal's Riot in 1624, he was tortured to death. When the people of Hamgyŏng Province later asked for his vindication, he was exonerated and enshrined in Ch'ŏngam Shrine in Puryŏng. He wrote *The Collected Works of Nongp'o*.

[360] Refers to the Pukkwan Sweepng Victory when General Chŏng Munbu defeated Kato's army and Kuk Kyŏngin, as well as Jurches at Kyŏngsŏng and Kilju, to reclaim Hamgyŏng Province. With three thousand volunteer soldiers, he defeated an army of 22,000 in the Battle of Paekt'ap.

[361] 楚懷王: A descendant of King Huai of Chu, he was renamed Emperor Yi and enthroned when Hsiang Yu founded the Chu dynasty at 208 BC. A symbolic leader of the anti-Qin group, he was killed by Hsiang Yu when the Qin dynasty was destroyed.

him to ruin.
When I think of the sorrow of this martyr and loyal subject,
my hair stands on end and tears fall.

During the Japanese invasion of Chosŏn in 1592, Kuk Sep'il rioted and surrendered to Japan. Chŏng Munbu, Commander-in-Chief of the North, subjugated them. Later he met with disaster because of his poem, "King Huai of the Chou dynasty."

169. *Please Don't Throw Stones at the Crows*

I ask, what do you think
of our beloved northern seaside?
When the crows kept cawing from the roof
the owner of the house came out with a stick to scare them
 away.
He threw stones at them—in vain.
The crows flew off then returned to caw louder.
An exile from the south felt sorry for them
and went into the yard to bow his head and weep.
"Owner of the house, please don't be so angry.
The crows in the woods know how to fulfill their filial
 duties.
They serve their parents, they're better than humans.
We should love them, not hate."

When the owner of my house drove the crows away, I wrote "A Song of Loving Crows" to teach him a lesson.

THINKING WINDOW VERSES

170. *Sibling Rocks*

I ask, what do you think
of our beloved northern seaside?
Two rocks are bowing to each as if they know the proprieties.
Is the one in front the older brother and the one behind the younger?
Because they stand as close together as siblings,
they haven't been worn away by wind or rain.
Names handed down through the ages are not preposterous:
the standing sibling rocks maintain their brotherly love.
Alas, what sins did I commit in my life
that I should live in a corner of the sky, separated from my siblings?
When I stand alone before the Nŭngsogak Pavilion,
pitiful tears moisten my cold sideburns, overwhelming me.

These odd-shaped sibling rocks, which contain a well, are twenty li from the fortress, where Commander Yi Kwangsŏp built a pavilion and called it Nŭngsogak.

171. *An Empty Promise to Yŏnhŭi*

I ask, what do you think
of our beloved northern seaside?
I have a house and some furrowed fields in my southern town,
with a fine landscape—mountains in back, water in front.
I promised Yŏnhŭi to buy green straw raincoats and bamboo hats
and enjoy the pleasures of farming for a hundred years,
working with my long plough while she hoed.
Most human plans come to nothing.
I recall my empty words and search my memory.
How can I fly back to Nakkyo
to keep my promise, pointing at Mt. Ullyong?[362]

---

[362] Another name for Mt. Ch'ŏnggye, which is in Puryŏng.

THINKING WINDOW VERSES

172. *To My Exiled Brother*

I ask, what do you think
of our beloved northern seaside?
During the five years I lived in the north,
I received three annual letters from Sŏwŏn.
A half year has passed since I came south.
He was exiled to the west, making it impossible to meet.
The Creator isn't just. Heaven isn't benevolent!
My brother, my brother, what crime did you commit on earth?
The judge re-examined the case—and separated us
by three thousand li to the north and south.
I hope you don't keep that in mind. Say nothing idle,
because a new king has ascended to the throne in this prosperous age.

I came to Chinhae this spring, and Sŏwŏn went into exile in Ch'osan.[363]

---

[363] A town on the North P'yŏngan Province border, by the bank of the Amnokkang River.

173. *Magpies of Chinhae*

I ask, what do you think
of our beloved northern seaside?
A flight of magpies suddenly gathered on the persimmon
    tree in my yard
and croaked *kkaak kkaak*, as if delivering good news.
I was startled by the sound, and with a deep sigh
I recalled the magpie chick in the eaves of my rented house
    in Puryŏng.
No news from morning until evening:
are Puryŏng magpies wise and Chinhae magpies foolish?
I heard that a strange magpie boarded a ship
and crossed the sea when my ancestor Noh was released
    from exile.
This poor descendant is stupid. Magpies aren't the same.
Magpies, what do you know croaking, *kkaak kkaak*?

Seven generations ago, during the reign of King Kwanghae, my ancestor Noh went into exile on Cheju Island and was released in 1623. Magpies are said to bear signs of good news. I wrote "A Poem of Singing Divine Magpies."

THINKING WINDOW VERSES

174. *Copper Paksan Censer*[364]

I ask, what do you think
of our beloved northern seaside?
Yŏnhŭi bought from a merchant in Sŏngch'ŏn
a delicately carved copper Paksan censer.
When they opened shops in Musan,
they promised to trade two nips of silver for ten of copper.
But when red gold was produced, not white,[365]
merchants brought these censers to sell instead.
Yŏnhŭi said, "There are times when money comes and
  goes.
It's useless to say silver is rare and copper is common."
Meanwhile this censer might have become junk.
I wonder who will burn a blue wick of sandalwood in it?

Sŏngch'ŏn Prefecture is in Kwansŏ Province. When Yu Sangnyang opened silver shops there, he recruited unruly boys, who vanished when copper was produced instead of silver.

---

[364] The name of a censer, with the shape of Mt. Pak engraved on top—a mythical lotus-shaped mountain in the sea. Originally it was a treasure of the Han dynasty, but imitations were made later.

[365] Here red gold means copper and white gold, silver.

175. *My Friendship with Sunjŏng*

I ask, what do you think
of our beloved northern seaside?
I met Sunjŏng briefly,
leaving before we had much time to talk.
I remember receiving his letters
from time to time, which made me happy.
But now all communication will be blocked.
Far better to have calculated thousands of possibilities.
When we parted, I told him
he should educate and encourage his children.
My Chunak was left alone, and my Hangak is sick.[366]
Through the long night my anxiety plagues me in this strange place.

When I was exiled to the south, I saw Sunjŏng at Chamsil of the Han River for just a minute. Sŏwŏn's son is Chunak and Sunchŏng's son is Hangak.

---

[366] Chun was Kim Ryŏ's nephew. Because Sunchŏng was apparently his relative from the same generation of his family tree, Hang would have been one generation behind him.

THINKING WINDOW VERSES

176. *Yŏngsanok's Calligraphy*

I ask, what do you think
of our beloved northern seaside?
Yŏngsanok's thin regular script resembles Kwangji's [367] calligraphy.
The elegant poem written on the green silk was Kyŏngbŏn's.[368]
"Jade water flows into the long lake of a clean autumn and a small boat is anchored in the deep, where lotus blooms.
Meeting her lover beyond the water and casting lotus seeds, she was caught by others and shamed for half a day."
There was another text written on white Akyŏ silk:[369]
Pigyŏng's [370] "A Thought at Dawn at Pyŏkkan'yŏk" in cursive running script.
I treasured these works, which were lost when I was transferred.

---

[367] The other name of Kwang Sehwang (1713-1791), a writer and calligrapher in the late Chosŏn dynasty; his penname was P'yo'ong. Seals and clerical scripts were his specialty.

[368] The other name of Hŏ Nansŏlhŏn (1563-1589). The poem is part of her "Song of Gathering Lotus Seeds."

[369] A high-quality silk produced in Yanting County, in China's Sichuan Province.

[370] The other name of Wen Tingyun (溫庭筠; 812–870), an important poet of the late Tang dynasty, who wrote many love poems. The full text of the poem, 碧磵驛曉思 is, "My dream is not fully awakened under the fragrant lamplight, and the Chu nation hangs from the edge of the sky. As the moon sets, the song of the cuckoo stops. Only mountain apricot flowers are full in the garden."

I wonder who will keep them in that desolate northern region.

Kwangji is P'yo'ong Kang Sehwang. Sanok was skilled in regular and cursive scripts. Once, I obtained her calligraphy: on the green silk was Hŏ Nansŏlhŏn's poem, and on the white silk was On Chŏnggyun's.

177. Generous and Clean Pak Ŭijung

I ask, what do you think
of our beloved northern seaside?
I really loved Kyogam[371] Pak of Tongch'on,
who was generous and pure-hearted.
He built a one-room hermitage by the red apricot woods,
and raised a half-kil tall tabernacle where white clouds lingered.
He treated his chronic disease with medicines
and practiced zazen, burning fragrant perfumes.
Last summer he went to Tanch'ŏn to buy medicines for me
and stayed downtown for several days.
How to enter the rock cave with him
and stroll leisurely, drinking dew and taking twilight for food?

When he was young, Pak Ŭijung was stricken with a strange disease, and so he devoted himself to buying medicines.

---

[371] 校勘: Kyogam was a fourth-ranked official in the Bureau of Diplomatic Documents. From the original note by Kim Ryŏ, we may surmise that Pak performed the role of inspector of publications in the Puryŏng government office.

178. *Writing an Epitaph for Hwangsu*[372]

I ask, what do you think
of our beloved northern seaside?
Student Hwang of Sunam was a descendant of a royal subject.
He was twenty years old, a pure, brilliant man,
who wanted to engrave his ancestor's feat
onto a clean hard stone from Hunyung.
He brought to my thatched house beef jerky and silk cloth
and begged me to write his epitaph and its seal script.
I'm ashamed of myself next to Paekkae,[373] an excellent writer.
How dare I write an epitaph for a turtle and a dragon-carved gravestone?
After a thousand years, when the water recedes and frost is cold,
who will read this epitaph on the cold mountain?

The student's name was Yunjung, and his other name was Sinji. His ancestor Hwangsu distinguished himself in war under General Chŏng Munbu and was later killed in battle along with Yi Kan.[374] *His other name was Ukyŏng.*

---

[372] A military general of the Chosŏn dynasty. See # 181.
[373] Cai Yong (蔡邕, 133~192) was an official and scholar in the Eastern Han dynasty. His other name was Bojie (伯喈). He was skilled in calligraphy, music, mathematics, and astronomy, and especially good at seal and clerical scripts. He invented Feibaishu (飛白書) style calligraphy.
[374] A regional military commander killed in battle against Jurchen in 1600. See # 91.

THINKING WINDOW VERSES

179. *Poems Hung on Puryŏng Guesthouse*

I ask, what do you think
of our beloved northern seaside?
Puryŏng Guesthouse has almost collapsed,
Eurasian red squirrels hide under the roof tiles, and
   chipmunks frequent the threshold.
Twenty-three poems hang on the walls.
Lord Hwang's[375] poem remains strong, Lord Yi's[376] is clean.
All the wood panels are covered with thick dark dust.
When will they be wrapped with blue silk and lodged in the
   tabernacle?
Though it's a different age, the feeling is the same, inspiring
   ideas.
When I try to compose with their rhymes, tears fall.
How dare I find a wooden board, apply multicolored paint,
and carve my own poem to hang beside old wise men's
   works?

Lord Hwang is Hwang Ho, a vice academic counsellor, and Lord Yi is Munhye Yi Annul. Their poems are carved on the board.

---

[375] 黃㦿 1604~1656, a literary man and scholar of the late Chosŏn dynasty. His other name was Chayu, and his penname was Manrang.

[376] 李安訥 1571~1637, a civil official and poet of the middle Chosŏn dynasty. His other name was Chamin, and his penname was Tongak. He was Hamgyŏng Provincial Governor in 1631. A skillful poet, he wrote at least 4379 poems and was a specialist of Tang poetry, often compared to Li Bai.

180. *Tonggwan Kim*

I ask, what do you think
of our beloved northern seaside?
Kim of Tonggwan[377] is seventy years old
and the bravest spirit in Kyŏngsŏng and Puryŏng.
With an imposing appearance—shiny face, dark beard—
he rides lightly over the rocky cliffs as if they were small hills.
Succeeding in the family business, he wrote *The Secret of the Medicine God*
and boasts the skill of Yang Yugi[378] whose arrows penetrated willow leaves.
A swift horse-like grandfather —like son, like grandson.
A family from Kangnŭng famous for generations.
Finally I know not to believe what people say.
All good springs have good sources, and lingzhi mushrooms have strong roots.

Army officer Kim's name is Sangni, his son is Hajin, and his grandson is Hyŏng'yu. His family business for generations was practicing medicine. He became an army officer in Tonggwan.

---

[377] A military camp in Chongsŏng, Hamgyŏng Province.
[378] 養由基 Yang Youji: A general in the Spring and Autumn periods. He is said to have hit the willow leaf accurately from one hundred steps.

THINKING WINDOW VERSES

181. *Brave Chubu*[379] *Hwang*

I ask, what do you think
of our beloved northern seaside?
Old people still talk about Chubu Hwang;[380]
brave and gallant, he was also an excellent marksman.
In Wŏn'gyo's[381] painting of a deer hunting scene,
blood-like rain spatters the forest red.
To the beat of a drum, he captured a Japanese general at Paekt'ap Field[382]
and put down barbarians at the border with three arrows aimed at Mijŏn Fortress.[383]
The king bestowed on him a golden saddle, a brave horse, and a red bow with a loose bowstring.
He looked magnificent on Chŏngt'amnyŏng Pass.[384]
In history books his fame will last forever.

Wŏn'gyo's painting was in Pang Sangch' ŏl's house. Hwang routed the Japanese invaders and captured barbarians at Mijŏn Fortress. King Sŏnjo bestowed on him a horse, a saddle, and a bow and arrows.

---

[379] 主簿: Keeper of records.
[380] Refers to Hwang Su, a military officer during Sŏncho's reign.
[381] The penname of Yi Kwangsa, a calligrapher during Yŏngjo's reign.
[382] A field south of Kilchu Fortress.
[383] A stone fortress twenty-six li east of Onsŏng.
[384] A pass west of Puryŏng.

182. *Jurchen Remains*

I ask, what do you think
of our beloved northern seaside?
Many headstones from the old house
are scattered around the fields of Osŏkch'on.
Even now farmers come across iron combs
while plowing the field in rain.
This was the site, between the mountains and the stream,
of the Jurchen prime minister's house, with its blue roof
    tiles and red banisters.
Last fall Wino, passing by the field,
stumbled on a copper container,
which looks like a tea kettle.
It has two handles, three legs, and a seal.
It takes one and a half bowls of water to fill it.

Osŏkch'on is the name of a village. The inscription on the seal says the kettle was made in Yuangongbao in the second year of Huangdao—i.e. in the time of Emperor Gaozong of Tang.

THINKING WINDOW VERSES

183. *Sir T'aeso, a Great Scholar of the North*

I ask, what do you think
of our beloved northern seaside?
Sir T'aeso had a pure soul,
he must have been O Rŭngja[385] in a previous life.
He's poor but likes to read books and behaves strangely.
Who but he is a great scholar in the north?
He has a hooked runny nose, a lantern jaw, a prominent temple,
and he wears a long overcoat cinched with a belt.
Once he visited me with Yi Paengnok,
clutching a book titled *Chŏngjumun*.[386]
He read it aloud then recited it again by heart,
relishing it like a delicacy.

T'aeso's name is Yi Chibaek; he is a student of Pusol[387] Yi Ham.
Yi Paengnok's other name is Yŏŭng; he is a student of Yu Chŏng.
The book refers to Sŏsayunsong,[388] *compiled by Yi Chae.*

---

[385] 於陵子 Yu Lingzi: Chen Zhongzi's other name. He was a famously righteous man.
[386] 程朱文 *Chengzhuwen*: A collection of writings by Cheng Hao, Cheng Yi, and Zhu Xi, Confucian scholars of the Song dynasty.
[387] 副率: The seventh-ranked military officer in charge of guarding the crown prince.
[388] 書社輪誦: A book with thirty-three texts by Song dynasty neo-Confucian scholars.

184. *Praising Devotion at the Immyŏng River*

I ask, what do you think
of our beloved northern seaside?
I have generally doubted Yu Ch'ŏlhan,[389]
but his study has accomplished something, Lord On-kong's[390] "integrity."
Nine out of ten memorials to the throne expose people's faults,
and Chijŏng met death after writing the "Chariot Cover Pavilion."[391]
If people use these as excuses in some future age,[392]
no good loyal slandered subject will survive.

---

[389] Refers to Liu Anshi (劉安世, 1048~1125), a Northern Song dynasty official. Ch'ŏlhan was his other name. A teacher from Sima Guang, famed for his admonitions, he was called "The Tiger in the Palace." He endured seven exiles but remained loyal—which was why Su Shi called him Ch'ŏlhan (Ironman).

[390] Refers to Sima Guang (司馬光, 1019~1086), a Confucian scholar-politician in the North Song dynasty. When Liu Anshi asked, "What is the key to fulfilling the heart?" he said, "Integrity."

[391] Refers to Cai Que (蔡確, 1037-1093), whose other name was Zhizheng (持正), a North Song dynasty literary figure. He wrote "Wandering the Chariot Cover Pavilion in a Summer Day." His political opponent, Wu Chuhou (吳處厚), accused him of slandering the king and comparing Empress Gao to Empress Wu. Empress Gao, infuriated, exiled him to Xinzhou, where he later died.

[392] Refers to the idiom that Tang, the first king of the Shang dynasty, felt shame after overthrowing Jie, the last Xia dynasty ruler. He said, "I fear that people will later use my action as an excuse."

THINKING WINDOW VERSES

Who ordered Nongp'o's death?[393]
How can Lord Kim and Lord Yi avoid shame?
Water weeps and flows absently for a thousand years
by the stronghold at the edge of the Immyŏng River, where
people fought fiercely.[394]

Nongp'o is the other name of Lord Ch'ung'ŭi, Chŏng Munbu. Lord Kim is Lord Munch'ung Kim Ryu, and Lord Yi is Lord Ch'ungjŏng Yi Kwi. They were powerful men at that time. Immyŏng is where Lord Ch'ung'ŭi won a great victory.

---

[393] See # 168.
[394] The place where a Korean volunteer army under Chŏng Munbu's command defeated the Japanese army during the Imjin War.

185. The Book of Mencius *Made of Three Different Calligraphies*

I ask, what do you think
of our beloved northern seaside?
I read *Mencius* from early on,
devoted to mastering its general meaning.
Because many types in the Government Printing Office
   were blurry,
we copied the book in a thin regular script on paper from
   the south.
My brother Sŏwŏn's calligraphy is rare even among the
   ancients
and Sunjŏng's style is truly extraordinary.
A copy was made with three different calligraphic styles;
the red and blue comments remain vivid.
Kanong borrowed it and still has not returned it.
I weep whenever I think about it.

Kanong is the other name of Im Hyŏngsu, a petty clerk of the prefecture, who was also a fine writer and calligrapher. He was Yŏnhŭi's cousin on the maternal side.

THINKING WINDOW VERSES

186. *The Literary Arts of Puryŏng Gisaengs*

I ask, what do you think
of our beloved northern seaside?
The hearts of the Puryŏng gisaengs are silk.
They help one other, they're good poets and drinkers.
Yŏngsanok's wit is like Sogun's,[395]
and Simhong's wisdom rivals To'on's.[396]
The owner of the Ch'ŏllyŏngnu Pavilion provided a place
for poetry competitions.
She was a heroine who led women warriors under silk
parasols.
The scholar who competed is greying now,
and an old Wonbi[397] can't draw his arrow even to raise a red

---

[395] 昭君 Chao-chun: Wang Qiang (Wang Chiang; 王牆, also 王檣 and 王嬙), commonly known by her stylistic name, Wang Zhaojun (Wang; 王昭君), one of the Four Beauties of ancient China. Born in Baoping Village, Zigui County (in current Hubei Province) in the Western Han dynasty, she was sent by Emperor Yuan to marry Xiongnu Chanyu Huhanye (呼韓邪) and establish friendly relations with the Han dynasty.

[396] 道韞 Daoyun: A niece of Xie An (謝安 320-385), a prime minister in the Eastern Jin dynasty. Asked to describe the falling snow, his cousin Xie Lang replied, "It is like salt scattered in the air." Xie Daoyun said, "It is not better than a pussy willow floating in the wind."

[397] A good archer. The idiom comes from the story that Yi Kwang (李廣, Li Guang), a Chinese general and archer in the Western Han dynasty, had the long arms of a monkey. Nicknamed "Flying General" by the Xiongnu, he fought primarily in the campaigns against the nomadic Xiongnu tribes north of China.

flag.[398]
I'd like to draw blue silk covers for you, hoping to discuss abstruse things and find some consolation in exile.

---

[398] 赤幟. Han Xin, a military general of the Han dynasty, tricked fighters from the Chu dynasty, lowering the Chu flag from their fortress and raising the Han's red flag to undermine the Chu soldiers' morale.

THINKING WINDOW VERSES

187. *Lord Yi, Who Governed Well*

I ask, what do you think
of our beloved northern seaside?
In political matters Lord Yi grasped the big picture,
practicing day and night the lessons of poetry and propriety.[399]
Devastated fishermen from the five ports were revitalized,
benefiting the poor monks of the six temples.
He trusted all to a Chamgonghyo-like[400] clerk on the Boards of Works.
Sly petty officials and wicked gisaengs moaned bitterly.
The empty kitchen in the government office was washed clean,
but the greedy provincial governor slandered him.
Both grey-haired old and wild-haired children gathered around the horse's head.
Lord Yi[401] didn't hesitate, wasting no time on tears.

---

[399] 詩禮之訓: A lesson in the home. Confucius asked his son, 鯉 Li, who lived with his mother, if he had been taught about poetry and propriety—which led him to teach his son a lesson.
[400] 岑公孝, Cen Gongxiao: a famously honest deputy to Cheng Jin (成瑨), Governor of Nanuang, who entrusted matters of state to him and enjoyed a life of leisure. His name was Cen Zhi (岑晊).
[401] Seems to refer to Yi Ch'angbae, Toho commander of Puryŏng. Falsely accused by Yi Pyŏngjŏng, Governor of Hamgyŏng Province, he was fired, flogged, and exiled to Anbyŏn. See #18, 21.

The five ports are Ch'ŏngjin, Yŏnjin, Anjin, Sŏrajin, and Sadongjin. The six temples are Yongyŏnsa, Paekryŏnsa, Yangsusa, Namsŏksa, Ch'ŏngnongsa, and Chŏngnongsa.

THINKING WINDOW VERSES

188. *Yi Kwangsa's Calligraphy of* Sangrye[402]

I ask, what do you think
of our beloved northern seaside?
I have seen many of Tobo's drafts,
and they match up with Ugun[403] and Chungnang.[404]
The one I just got is amazing.
Not even one thin stroke went wrong.
When I studied the silkworm dung-like characters,
they resembled ants or scorpions crawling over the earth.
In those days people used or adapted Lord Zhu Xi's *Family Ceremony*,
following the example of the Munwŏn edition.[405]
Ah, this draft is a rare treasure,
where you can glimpse the marvelous calligraphy in *Yellow Court Classic.*[406]

Tobo copied out Funeral Ceremony *in its entirety. The book was compiled by Lord Zhu Xi and Sakye. At that time, an expurgated version, small as one's palm, was kept in Tamsu's house.*

---

[402] 喪禮: A chapter about funeral rites in *Family Ceremony* (家禮).
[403] 右軍 Youjun: Refers to Wang Xizhi, a Jun dynasty writer and official best known for his mastery of Chinese calligraphy.
[404] 中郎 Zhonglang: Refers to Cai Yong (蔡邕). An Eastern Han dynasty official and scholar, skilled in calligraphy.
[405] 文元本: Refers to *Karyejipram* (家禮輯覽), which Kim Changsaeng, a scholar in the middle period of Chosŏn dynasty, revised and annotated. Munwŏn is his posthumous title.
[406] 黃庭經 *The Yellow Court Classic*, a Taoist meditation text. Here it means a draft of the text, which was said to have been written by Wang Xizhi.

189. *Letters from My Brother and Brother-in-law*

I ask, what do you think
of our beloved northern seaside?
Nyusan[407] pleaded over and over in a short letter,
and my brother Sŏwŏn sent word to be alert.
I vomited daily, had diarrhea,
and shamed myself before Wŏnsŏng[408] and Noch'ŏm.[409]
I cherished them, kept their works in my hands for three
 years
until they blurred, shed tears in sorrow.
Here in the south, contagious disease is rampant.
The damp, dim twilight and poisonous vapor roil the heavy
 sea.
I lie on a pillow among ripe persimmons,
a fishy smell blocks my nose, boils swell on my legs.

Nyusan Yi Ikji sent me a letter, encouraging me with Tongp'a's Yŏng'oe poems. My brother Sŏwŏn also warned me with an anecdote about Wŏnsŏng's pilgrimage to the seven towns.

---

[407] The penname of Yi Usin, a Confucian scholar in the late Chosŏn period. His other name was Ikchi, and his father was Kim Ryŏ's father-in-law. Kim Ryŏ loved and respected him from his youth. He wrote *Nyusan Literary Works* and *Posthumous Works of Susan*.
[408] Refers to Liu Anshi (劉安世 1048-1125), a Northern Song dynasty celebrity. Falsely accused and exiled several times, he returned home safely. Upright in spirit, he was never swayed by either life or death, fortune or misfortune.
[409] 老瞻 means an old Chach'om, the other name of Su Shi, a Chinese writer, poet, painter, calligrapher. His penname was Dongpo. His many exiles deepened his writing.

190. *Famous Doctors beyond Mach'ŏllyŏng Ridge*

I ask, what do you think
of our beloved northern seaside?
Yujŏng's book on acupuncture is marvelous.
His disciple Yŏŭng's dexterity resembled that of his master.
Who are the most famous doctors now?
I heard old Yuk visited old Hŏ for a lesson.
Yŏŭng's medical skills have a clear origin,
and he is better known north of Mach'ŏllyŏng Pass.
Kim at Tongkwan[410] lacked courage,
hesitating to prescribe medications.
He couldn't cure my disease last summer.
Later I met Yŏŭng, who applied acupuncture on my stomach.

Old Yuk's name is Yisŏn. I wrote The Story of Scholar Yuk *separately. My friend Hŏgak's other name is Chakyŏng, and he is a recluse.*

---

[410] Refers to Kim Sangni. See #180.

KIM RYŎ

191. *Yŏnhŭi Came to See Me on a Snowy Day*

I ask, what do you think
of our beloved northern seaside?
A north wind blew, freezing the valley,
and snowflakes big as cushions buried the cold pavilion.
I lay in my empty bed, worrying.
Weather strips fluttered on the paper window full of holes.
Suddenly there was tapping on the stone road—
Yŏnhŭi walking over the snow to knock on my twig door.
With a black gourd bottle in one hand,
she sat close to the brazier to heat the wine.
Tipsy, we sang until our earlobes were warm.
Where in the world can I find a better person than her?

THINKING WINDOW VERSES

192. *Lord Kim Hŭi's High Virtue*

I ask, what do you think
of our beloved northern seaside?
How sad! Virtuous Lord Kim from Yŏnsan
lived up to our expectations working for three royal courts.
It was I who was wrong about the Ginkgo Altar,[411]
but Lord Kim, an older man of virtue, didn't punish me.
I tried to attack him for ten years, with a lance in my hand,
and he never seemed to mind, just as ice melts and clouds
    disappear.
Age meant nothing in his friendships,
and he accepted the king's edict, his works and service
    being recognized.
When I wailed for him in front of the San'gosujangnu
    Pavilion,
even the animals cried through the night.

Lord Kim's penname is Hŭi and his other name is Sŏnji. When he directed the National Academy, I argued with him over a certain issue. Ten years later, we resolved our argument. This is recorded in Ch'imjŏllok.

---

[411] Originally a ginkgo platform where Confucius taught. Here it refers to Sŏngkyunkwan, the National Confucian Academy, where Kim Ryŏ studied and Kim Hŭi was the headmaster.

193. In the House of P'unghŏn[412] Yi

I ask, what do you think
of our beloved northern seaside?
Autumn came and red-leaved trees were everywhere.
I slowly climbed the steep eastern slope of Mt. Ch'ŏnggye.
When I saw the stone bridge, a horse was heading south.
I looked down at the green, deep pond at P'unghŏn Yi's house.
A maple tree rose majestically by the pond,
and the frost-bitten leaves seemed red as drunks.
When I stood with my goosefoot cane under the tree,
the owner of the house opened the door to greet me warmly.
After drinking heartily with a gourd dipper,
we parted at the twig gate at twilight.

P'unghŏn's name is Hŭngp'al and his other name is Inwŏn. He is Paengnok's elder cousin.

---

[412] A clerk on the local government advisory committee.

THINKING WINDOW VERSES

194. *Fabrics of Kwanbuk*

I ask, what do you think
of our beloved northern seaside?
The people of Kwanbuk always brag about Pukye cloth.[413]
I too fell in love with this white silk.
Ŭngya gave me two p'il[414] of it;
even cicada's wings could not match such beauty.
I showed it off to Yŏnhŭi,
who compared it to the one on her loom, laughing.
"It's coarse and weak," she said. "How can I gauge what it's worth?"
Then she wove by herself eleven sae[415] of fabric on her loom.
I don't think even the so-called twenty sae fabric is better than this.

Among the fabrics of Kwanbuk, the one from Chongsŏng is considered the best; among the fabrics of Chongsŏng, the one from Pukye is the best. But it falls short of Yŏnhŭi's.

---

[413] The fabric produced in Pukye, a town in Chongsŏng.
[414] A traditional measure of length, one p'il is about twelve meters.
[415] A traditional unit of measured for counting threads. One sae is eighty threads; therefore eleven sae means eight hundred and eighty threads. The number of sae was an important measure of the quality and beauty of any fabric.

195. *Pak Insŏp with Many Blessings*

I ask, what do you think
of our beloved northern seaside?
I envy Yangsa[416] Pak, my neighbor to the west,
who has more blessings than anyone.
His eldest son plows stony fields with an ox,
his young son-in-law is a fine bow hunter with sharp arrows,
and his grandchildren read Confucian canons and history books,
associating with scholars and eminent dignitaries.
He grows millet in twenty furrows and reaps ten mal from every furrow.
The jars are full of the chrysanthemum-fragrant wine he makes every spring.
He gets drunk as a fish in the fall
and lies spread-eagled under the autumn-colored pear tree.

Pak Insŏp's grandfather, Hŭnggyu, was on Yangsajae's directorate. His son is Ch'angdon and his son-in-law is Kim Ch'angmun.

---

[416] A temporary bureau for training scholars. It also refers to the directorate of the bureau.

196. *Chang Aeae and Yŏnhŭi, Chivalrous Female Fighters of the North*

I ask, what do you think
of our beloved northern seaside?
Who were the chivalrous women north of Mach' ŏllyŏng?
There was Hyŏllyŏng's sister before Yŏnhŭi.
She served Sir Wŏn'gyo with a towel and a comb,
preparing food for him like Tŏkyo.[417]
When by royal order Wŏn'gyo was transferred to a southern island,
she followed him in secret and died on the shore.
Our society grows more perverse, vicious slanders everywhere,
and Yŏnhŭi is locked up in prison, bound with a rope.
History knows no such atrocities.
With a deep sigh, I shed tears, stifling the sound of my weeping.

When Wŏn'gyo was exiled to Sinji Island, Ms. Chang followed him and died there. When I was arrested, Yŏnhŭi was sent to the prison in the fortress captured by Yi Pyŏngjŏng.

---

[417] 德耀: Meng Guan of the Late Han dynasty. Tŏgyo was her other name. She came from a rich family but at her husband's suggestion she lived humbly, discarding her fancy clothes and wearing a hairpin made of thorns. She prepared food for him as a sign of respect.

197. *The Wild Conventions of Kwanbuk*

I ask, what do you think
of our beloved northern seaside?
The wild customs of Kwanbuk are well known,
but it was wilder during Provincial Governor Yi's reign.
Chesŏng's wickedness had already been uncovered.
The world changed, and Sin Hongkyŏng was imprisoned.
We have parents and brothers in this life,
and I'm wary of hot-blooded people.
The governor received baby ginseng, soft deer antlers,[418]
and northern horses, and instigated these atrocities.
Later, the king's special envoy came to examine this imprisonment
and Chonghwa was struck by an arrow in the dark.

Honggyŏng is from Musan. I wrote "The Details of Mr. Chang and Yi's Imprisonment and the Full Account of Honggyŏng's Imprisonment" separately. Chonghwa is Yi Chesŏng's son.

---

[418] Ginseng and deer antlers are precious ingredients in Asian herbal medicine.

THINKING WINDOW VERSES

198. *Chang Chŏngse* [419] *Unfairly Treated by the Provincial Administration*

I ask, what do you think
of our beloved northern seaside?
Chang Chŏngse's hair turned grey,
but he reawakened decaying customs with his righteous words and deeds.
Like boiling water, with his grave heart and strong will,
he raged against the evil deeds of others.
Every scholar hid from the quarrel between Mr. Chang and Mr. Yi,
which he alone fought with his own body.
Instead of being rewarded, he was falsely charged,
and the provincial administration threatened to butcher him.
Oh, it would be better to fall into Muwa[420]
or keep his body clean in the depths of the sea.

Mr. Chang and Mr. Yi refer to Yi Chesŏng and his brother-in-law Chang Tuuk.

---

[419] According to #16, Chang Chŏngse was the head of peddlers. See also the note to #56.
[420] Refers to the state of never waking from sleep. The word comes from *The Book of Odes*: "All troubles invade me, and I wish to fall asleep and never wake."

199. *Yŏnhŭi's Words*

I ask, what do you think
of our beloved northern seaside?
When autumn rains fell and the sound of the wooden bat
beating the felting cloth on the fulling block rang cold,
Yŏnhŭi and I talked late into the night.
She argued for the importance of having good friends,
gazing sadly at the fading lamplight:
"Is there even one in a million
who won't betray friends in life and death?"
I felt ashamed, as if an iron needle had stung my body.
Though others betray me, I will not do the same.
These words I will recite three times a day for the rest of my life.

After hearing this, I never thought of betraying anyone, despite the many unexpected disasters I endured. I am greatly indebted to Yŏnhŭi for this.

200. In Namsŏk Valley

I ask, what do you think
of our beloved northern seaside?
Several li of valley stretched out under Mt. Namsŏk;
the valley was deep and rocky, and the stream meandered.
A pine tree with a dark green trunk and old boughs, by a rock
near the stream, might have harbored a baby dragon.
I went daily to clutch the boughs and weep,
and my bloody tears streamed down, cleaning the gaps between the rocks.
Since June 1800, the heart of this lonely
vassal at the edge of the sky has steadily burned.[421]
I went to the pine tree every morning and evening,
my embittered grudge congealing to thicken the world.

Every day after King Chŏngjo's death, I went to the valley to clutch boughs and weep. Only Scholar Kim Hŭiik followed me daily.

---

[421] King Chŏngjo's death on June 28, 1800 (lunar calendar) dashed Kim Ryŏ's hopes for his exile to end and heightened the prospect of severe punishment by the Party of Principle 僻派.

201. Ch'angryŏl Shrine

I ask, what do you think
of our beloved northern seaside?
My failure to visit Ŏrangp'o[422] for five years,
having come to the end of the northern waters, is regrettable.
With excellent skill, Ullo composed a text,
Hansa wrote a poem praising Ch'angnyŏl, and they recited their works.
The Mukye Lake is clean and calm, the rocks look ancient.
A shrine commemorating Ch'angnyŏl stands deep in the mountains.
I still remember the battlefield from our victory then:
soldiers with white headbands and moss-covered spears encircling the waterside.
How can I find a way to visit it
and look for traces of the sage I imagined?

Ŏrang and Mukye are placenames in Kyŏngsŏng. A shrine for Lord Ch'ungŭi stands in Mukye. Executive of the Royal Secretariat Chancellery, Nam Kuman,[423] and Minister Hong Yanghan[424] composed texts about this historical site.

---

[422] A port southeast of Kyŏngsŏng, Hamgyŏng Province.
[423] Nam Kuman (1629-1711): A late Chosŏn dynasty writer. His other name was Ullo, and his penname was Yakch'ŏn. As provincial governor, he solidified the defense of the border. He wrote *The Collected Works of Yakch'ŏn*.
[424] Hong Yangho (1724-1802): A late Chosŏn dynasty writer. Yanghan was his childhood name, Hansa his other name, and Yigye his penname. He was District Magistrate of Kyŏnghŭng, Minster of Personnel, and First Academician. He wrote *The Collected Works of Yigye*.

THINKING WINDOW VERSES

202. *Scholar Ch'oe's Poems*

I ask, what do you think
of our beloved northern seaside?
Scholar Ch'oe of Sŏkpong is simple and sincere.
He bested his classmates with his superb writing skills.
After finishing a long piece, he would recite it
in a voice that sounded like rolling jade balls.
Last summer, riding his black ox backwards,
he brought melons to me through the rain.
All the poems inside his sleeves were excellent,
as if a black dragon played with a pearl ball.
He confessed to writing *Song of Tan'gun* when he was young,
rhyming it with obscure letters like *chong* (樅) and *kong* (灨).

Sŏkpong is a placename. Scholar Choe's name is Yubang; his other name is Sinbo. He studied Zuo Zhuan (Spring and Autumn Annals) *under me and wrote in his youth* Song of Tan'gun, *using all the letters in the letter song (送) rhyming system.*

203. *A Cedar Stationary Case*

I ask, what do you think
of our beloved northern seaside?
A beautiful cedar tree on T'anggok grew almost as high as
the clouds.
It was so gnarled and twisted no inking line could be drawn
of it.
Like an ancient rock, its trunk twisted to the right, its
branches to the left:
a deep hole made in the colorful halo of the sky.
A skilled artisan shaved and dug it out to make this case:
you can put brushes in it or place it on a bough to use as a
paper cabinet.
When Ilhong pasted bamboo to it,
it lost its original form and looked unnatural.
Now I live in a rented house in the south,
worrying that it will wallow in the dusty desk.

T'anggok is a placename where there is a deep spring. Ilhong is Kwon Ch'an, a clerk in the local administration.

204. *Terribly Cold*

I ask, what do you think
of our beloved northern seaside?
Snow fell for ten days in a row in January,
cattle froze to death, crows and magpies disappeared.
The whole world was overturned, the north wind howled.
Elderly people sighed, calling it a catastrophe.
"There was a huge snowstorm in the spring of 1776.
Who knows what kind of disaster will befall us this time?"
No market was open outside the fortress for ten days,
and nine travelers froze to death.
A heaven-sent prodigy, young Kim, died suddenly.
It still makes me sad to think of that boy.

Old people say the snow of 1800 was the worst since 1776. The young boy's name was Sangdong, and he was unusually gifted. He left his village and froze to death in the snow.

205. Scroll with Poem and Painting

I ask, what do you think
of our beloved northern seaside?
A silver scroll with poetic phrases singing of the moon,
Who wrote it? Yŏngsanok.
There were eight people on that outing:
five men and some ladies.
Blue rocks soared to the sky,
where we ground ink in the moonlight to write poems.
An introduction was added to the poems written in archaic, square,
semi-cursive, and cursive styles, and Noh Simhong's painting was marvelous.
You should take care of it. Don't show it to just anybody.
This scroll is a rare treasure in the world.

In San'gosujangdae Pavilion Tamsu, Pak Sŏngsin, Ŭngya Kang Sangguk, Konso Nam Hŭngyu, Hŭiik Kim Hyŏngyu, Yŏnhŭi, Yŏngsanhong, Noh Simhong, and I enjoyed the moonlight. The poems and documents are in The Record of Yŏnhŭi's Words and Deeds.

THINKING WINDOW VERSES

206. *Famous Families in Puryŏng*

I ask, what do you think
of our beloved northern seaside?
Which family is the most powerful in Puryŏng?
The Hwang, Pak, Ch'a, and Chŏng families have declined.
Nowadays the Kim and Chang families are flourishing,
along with the Sinnong Kang family in Ori.
Kang's seven children are all quick and brilliant—
Ŭngya is the best and Sŏngun is excellent.
Sin'guk is a future pillar of the country.
When I look at them, all three have great talent.
It's all due to our king's wise, deep, and lovely virtue.

Hwang, Pak, Ch'a, Chŏng are famous families in Puryŏng. Kim Húiik's family and Chang Paingnŭng are also well-known. Ŭngya's elder cousin Sin'guk's other name is Chusin and Myŏngguk's other name is Sŏng'un.

KIM RYŎ

207. *Yi Tanha's[425] Appealing Letter*

I ask, what do you think
of our beloved northern seaside?
Chancellor Yi's heart was sparkling clean.
Song Uam's support was not just empty words.
Who cares about the things of other people?
You alone sent an appeal to the palace.
One hundred years after countless slanders caused a loyal servant
to be put to death, he was revenged solely by your efforts.
Flowers bloomed like clouds in front of the Ch'angnyŏlsa shrine,[426]
in the moonlight the Ch'ongnyongdang shrine house[427]
shone like white silk.
Northern elderly people still praise you
and weep, their throats choked, deeply moved.

Lord Yi's name was Tanha; his other name was Kyeju, and his penname was Oejae. Uam Song Siyŏl praised Yi Tanha for writing a letter of appeal, with a pure clean heart, to satisfy a grudge held by Chŏng Munbu. Ch'ongnyongdang is in front of the shrine.

---

[425] A seventeenth-century Confucian scholar and government official promoted to the first-vice premiership. He wrote many books, including *Pukkwanji*.
[426] A shrine to the volunteer army leader, Chŏng Munbu, in Ŏrang, Northern Hamgyŏng Province.
[427] A house in the Ch'angnyŏlsa shrine, built by Yi Tanha when he was a military commander in the north.

208. *Kwanbuk and Yŏngnam*

I ask, what do you think
of our beloved northern seaside?
Heaven divided Kwanbuk and Yŏngnam.
They say the south is for sages, the north for the Mohe
  people.
But the north is much better than the south,
judging from my experience of wandering here and there.
You cannot scoop up water from the Yellow River with a
  small bowl
or move seawater with a decrepit basket.
I may not be wise in the ways of the world,
but I, Tamjŏng, know that close attention may reveal many
  strange things.
I hope to recruit and place wise officials throughout the
  north and south
so they can make the flippant ways of the world more
  virtuous.

209. *Copper Brush Handle*

I ask, what do you think
of our beloved northern seaside?
A man on Mt. Suyang made a copper brush handle.
Who gave it to me? Oh T'aekkil.
It is made of copper, with three columns;
the top is a brush case, the base, a Chinese ink container.
The gold thread-tied tip of the brush is in the handle,
and the ink comes through a hole in the brush case,
  touching the tip.
Because a master artisan put his heart and soul into it, it's
  best
to tie it to one's cloth and go sightseeing.
The benefits of a brush can save the whole world.
One day I will write an ode to a brush.

Suyang is the name of a mountain in Chongsŏng. T'aekkil's other name is Chunghwa, and he learned Annotations on The Book of Odes *under me.*

THINKING WINDOW VERSES

210. *My Brother's Warning*

I ask, what do you think
of our beloved northern seaside?
Sŏwŏn is a wise brother with foresight.
He sent me a letter with a warning:
Quoting Tongp'a's phrase, "Hidden dragon,"[428]
he said to beware of poems that inspire disaster.
I thought, "Doesn't heaven determine my life span?
How can poetry shape my fortune and misfortune?"
Neglecting his advice, I met with disaster,
narrowly escaping death this spring at the execution site.
Better from here on out to burn my poetry manuscripts,
shut my mouth, pass my time in silence.

This spring, Yi Pyŏngjŏng snooped on dozens of my regulated verses, and sent a fabricated report to the king. This event is recorded in Kamdamsokki.

---

[428] Tongp'a (Dongpo in Chinese) was Sosik's (Su Shi) penname. "Hidden dragon" (蟄龍) comes from his poem, "Ode to a Korean Spindle Tree": "The root is not curved until it reaches Hades, and only the hidden dragon in the world knows it."

211. *A Book for Studying and Editing* Exegesis on a Record of Reflection[429]

I ask, what do you think
of our beloved northern seaside?
My late father divided his *Exegesis on a Record of Reflection*
into many thin volumes to read and memorize.
Lord Sumong pointed out dubious passages,
and Lord Sakye[430] and Lord Uam[431] completed it.
My father studied and edited it, adding and subtracting,
gathering similar items into clusters, leaving no missing words.
I, his unworthy son, dared to add punctuation marks
and devoted myself to reducing the number of mistakes.
Scholar Kang and I continued teaching and compiled a book
to pass on our teaching properly.

Sumong is Lord Munsuk Chŏngyŏp, and his other name is Sihoe.
Scholar Kang is Ŭngya.

---

[429] Refers to Chŏngyŏp's *Exegesis on a Record of Reflection* (Xiansi Lu, 近思錄) compiled by the South Zhu Xi and Lu Zuqian and published in 1661.
[430] Kim Changsaeng's penname.
[431] Song Siyŏl's penname.

THINKING WINDOW VERSES

212. *My Heart Honoring Ch'angnyŏlsa*

I ask, what do you think
of our beloved northern seaside?
Near Ŏrang Port in Mukye, there is a place
where the beach has receded, and a lake opened.
How could the cloud dragon secure a hundred cedars
to weave a thatched house with a few rafters deep in the mountains?
Yi Songam, a learned and virtuous scholar, tried hard
to honor Army Commander Chŏng's brave spirit and heroism.
Minister Min was splendid in appearance and attitude.
The Kwanbuk people inscribe their gratitude on their hearts.
Such customs have not yet gone extinct.
In admiration they gaze at the green mountain.

Songam is Minor Inspector Yi Chaehyŏng,[432] a literary figure under Nongam Kim Ch'anghyŏp. Ch'angnyŏl shrine, which Lord Munch'ung Min Chŏngjung built, is in Mukye, Kyŏngwon.

---

[432] Yi Chaehyŏng (1665-1741). A late Chŏsun period writer. His other name was Kahoe, and his penname was Songam. Born in Kyŏngsŏng, Hamgyŏng Province, he studied under Nongam Kim Ch'anghyŏp when he commanded the army in 1685. One of the most famous Neo-Confucianism scholars in Pukkwan, he wrote *Collected Works of Songam*.

KIM RYŎ

213. *Healing Methods of the Puryŏng People*

I ask, what do you think
of our beloved northern seaside?
Kwanbuk people treat diseases like enemies,
coaxing runaway soldiers to defeat them.
Last winter, Kijung said I should reverse my yin and yang
    to treat this illness
while Taesim wandered helplessly around,
saying I was impatient and extravagant.
They put a double dose of astragalus in my Yŏngbo soup,
which made my neck stiff and left me coughing and
    burping.
But after three bowls of soup my fever subsided.
When I got up early in the morning and asked for porridge,
they cheered—and lamented my partial recovery.

Kijung is Ch'usu, Yŏngha's cousin. Taesim is Ch'unghwa Kim Hajin, a local clerk. Yŏngbo is an herbal potion.

THINKING WINDOW VERSES

214. *Treacherous Clerks in the Provincial Administration*

I ask, what do you think
of our beloved northern seaside?
Who is most triumphant among the provincial governor's henchmen?
Sunmin is wicked and Kyŏngbo is jealous.
They fatten themselves on the people's sweat and blood
while the Saengwhang [433] and the cross-flute sound continuously by the sea.
Kunmyŏng and Puyong fight each other,
and Kyŏngbo enjoys a good time with lewd Murŭngch'un.
A treacherous fox and a wicked kyŏng,[434] assuming the power of a tiger,
hire and fire dependents like servants.
I wish I could summon Hŏ Chin'gun[435] to wield his divine sword
and behead this gang of comets.[436]

Sunmin is Yŏnggyo[437] Han Sunmin, and Kunmyŏng is his cousin.

---

[433] A mouth organ with seventeen bamboo pipes.
[434] The name of a beast that resembles a tiger with a smaller body. It is said to catch red-throated divers.
[435] 許眞君 Xu Yujin, refers to 許遜 Xu Xun (239-374), a Jin dynasty Taoist priest.
[436] In ancient times, a comet was viewed as foreboding, since it invaded the Purple Forbidden and Heavenly Market enclosures, constellations that symbolized the king.
[437] Military officer attached to the local administration or military base.

Kyŏngbo is Chŏin[438] *Won Kyŏngbo. Kyŏngbo had affairs with Gisaeng Murŭngch'un, and Kunmyŏng with Puyong.*

---

[438] Local clerk in charge of communications between local authorities and counties.

THINKING WINDOW VERSES

215. *A Handwritten Copy of* The Book of Odes

I ask, what do you think
of our beloved northern seaside?
Petty official Kang in Pyŏkkye[439] copied *The Book of Odes*,
which Sunjŏng collated and my brother Sŏwŏn corrected.
This book was a great help to me.
I have read and studied it more than a thousand times.
I recall receiving at the age of twenty "Sunt'ong"[440] at Sunduilch'a.
Konso enjoyed reading "Xiang Shu"[441] in *The Book of Odes*.
He was worthy of the phrase: a man of deep propriety.
I was in no hurry to give him the book.
No scholar in Kwanbuk could match him.

When my late father worked as the local magistrate in Changsu, I asked petty official Kang to copy The Book of Odes. *Sunduilch'a refers to chŏn'gang.*

---

[439] A placename in Changsu, Cholla Province.
[440] A recital contest among the scholars at Sŏngkyunkwan held in the dining room on the 16th day of every even month. Sundu refers to November, and chŏn'gang was a test of learned scholars before the king, in which they recited by heart passages from *Three Classics* or *Five Classics*, determined by whichever thin paper stick was picked.
[441] "Xiang Shu" in *Odes of Yong*. The poems in this section lament the loss of propriety: "Look at a rat—it has its limbs. But a man should be without dignity of demeanor. If a man has no dignity of demeanor, what should he do but die?" *Shijing, Book of Odes: Bilingual Edition, English and Chinese* 詩經: *Classic of Poetry, Book of Songs* (Kindle Locations 1301-1305). Lionshare Media. Kindle Edition.

KIM RYŎ

216. Mr. Sŏ, the Youngest Son

I ask, what do you think
of our beloved northern seaside?
Among the three brothers of my renter, Mr. Sŏ,
the youngest was good at riding horses and wrestling.
When he traveled as a young man to Kwansŏ Province for business,
his silk saddle and embroidered flap shone brilliantly.
But now he is bankrupt, greying,
and busily hoeing and plowing the field.
His two older brothers were unfriendly to me,
but he and I remained so close
I gave him my old pants and a gown.
I still miss him.

Sŏ Myŏngse, Myŏngwŏn, and Undae, were brothers. Last winter I gave Undae my old pants and a gown.

217. Sir Yujŏng's Cucumber Field

I ask, what do you think
of our beloved northern seaside?
Sir Yujŏng's cucumber field with scattered stones and tiles
is ten li from the east gate of the fortress.
When I look at Yŏnhui's picture of the well fields,[442]
I see sixty-four roads as clear as the lines of my own hand.
Public and private fields in one hundred mu[443] must be a Chu system.
The picture of p'almun'gijŏng[444] is rightly deduced from Hŏnwŏn.
Cucumbers have been planted in that field for about fifty years;
crows and magpies damaged less than eighty percent, but hornworm devastated all.

---

[442] 井田: A Chinese land distribution method in the Zhou dynasty. A square land was divided into nine identical sections, eight private outer sections and a communally-owned inner one.
[443] Mu is a unit of land. Six square cheok is one po, and one hundred po is one mu (one cheok is about 30.3 cm). In the well field system, 100 mu was allotted to each man.
[444] P'almun: eight gates in the eight camps picture. The eight camps were devised by the Yellow Emperor (whose birthplace was Hŏnwon, Xuanyuan) and consisted of one set of four camps—sky, earth, wind, and cloud—and another set of four camps—dragon, bird, tiger, and snake. Zhuge Liang (諸葛亮) spread this eight-camps model to the four corners, creating sixty-four military camps. The dragon, tiger, bird, and snake camps were called Sagi (四奇) and the rest were called Sajŏng (四正). Thus Kijŏng means this saki and sajŏng. Jŏng means to build a stronghold and fight hand-to-hand, and ki means to hide or ambush.

From the Ŏbok waterside[445] to Kich'ŏn valley
the contributions of old and young alike are piled in many layers.

The Kich'ŏn valley beyond the east gate was Sir Yujŏng's cucumber field. Yŏnhŭi embroidered a picture of well fields in the eight camps. This is recorded in Sŏlgoyŏngŏn.

---

[445] Ŏbok (魚腹, Yufu): From to *The Book of Jin*, "Zhuge Liang collected stones on the sand marsh of Yufu to make eight lines (八行), and the distance between the lines was two jang (about six m).

THINKING WINDOW VERSES

218. *Five Tiger-like Generals*

I ask, what do you think
of our beloved northern seaside?
When the Japanese army invaded in 1592,
running wild as beasts, our seven provinces were stomped
 on
like the flesh of fish, pools filled with blood,
and for eight years our king was forced to live in Ŭiju.
What power kept the north safe?
Rumors of Chŏng Munbu's volunteer army swirled in the
 East Sea.
Five tiger-like generals worked together,
 their righteous loyalty and upright spirits shining
 majestically.
Strong honorable souls, you will be chief ghosts,
with the old shrine on the riverside hill standing high above.

The five tiger-like generals—Special Army officer Kang Munu, Myriarch Yi Hŭidang, and Scholars Yi Pongsu, Chi Talwŏn, and Ch'oe Paech'ŏn—are enshrined in Ch'angnyŏlsa.

219. Seven Warriors of the North

I ask, what do you think
of our beloved northern seaside?
Three imposing men from the Ch'a family,
tiger-like descendants of nobility—
who on earth could fight a million troops
in the horrendous Japanese invasion of 1592?
They dashed toward the Japanese general like thunderbolts
and beheaded him, saving our county.
The Kim and Pak brothers performed remarkable feats,
they are also descendants of brave generals from the north.
A sacred aura is circling forever
around Sŏngmun rock on which they washed their arrows.

The three Cha brothers of Ŭngnin, Tŭkto, Tŏkhong, Kim Kyŏng, Kim Chŏn, Pak Kŭkkŭn, and Pak Inbŏm accomplished remarkable feats under Chŏng Munbu. Sŏngmun is a placename.

220. *Unfair Imprisonment*

I ask, what do you think
of our beloved northern seaside?
What I most regret is the terrible suffering I endured.
Where is the pure land in this world?
The fire at the fortress gate reached the fish in the pond.
Hardship changed the minds of the townspeople.
The boundless world is vast, but its net is very fine.
What sins have the men and women in Puryŏng committed?
Poor indeed is the Hwangmun Puksi Prison![446]
All my nine kinship families were interrogated, and my friends suffered.
Kongp'o[447] was killed because of Changgŏm,
and I'm ashamed before Habok,[448] who bit his tongue and pounded his chest.

---

[446] 黃門北寺 The Huangmen North Temple Prison: Puksi was the name of the Hwangmun police station prison in the East Han period, where high officials and ministers were interrogated. It was called the North Temple Prison because it is in the north.
[447] 孔褒, Kong Bao: A man in the Late Han period acquainted with Changgŏm (張儉, Zhang Jian). When Changgŏm visited him in exile, he was hidden by teenage brother Kongyung (孔融, Kong Rong). When this was discovered, Kongp'o, Kong Bao, and their mother were interrogated—and confessed. Emperor Ling (靈帝) had Kongp'o executed.
449 During Han Emperor Ling's reign, he criticized the affairs of state and incurred the hatred of powerful eunuchs. When the Emperor issued an arrest warrant for him, he escaped to the Imnyŏ Mountains (林慮, Linlinyi) and disguised himself to work in a blacksmith shop.

This spring, Yi Pyŏngjŏng sent a military cadre and arrested one hundred people, including Ch'a Namkyu and Yŏnhŭi, with a forged warrant from Tongjo.[449] *He punished them unfairly.*

---

[449] The dowager queen's house east of the main palace—e.g., the king's grandmother, Queen Chŏngsun (her maiden surname was Kim), who was the regent behind her veil.

THINKING WINDOW VERSES

221. *Petty Official Pak Living in the West*

I ask, what do you think
of our beloved northern seaside?
The petty officials in Puch'un[450] were foolish,
but I grew close to Pak, who lived west of my house.
Official Pak was sincere,
a lifelong lover of scholarship and wine.
His brothers were clumsy,
but he wasn't vulgar.
When he was tortured on my account,
he remained perfectly calm, as if unafraid of death.
When spring wine ripened in the jar,
he would call me over the wall to drink with him.

The petty official's name is Ch'undŭk; his brothers are Ch'undal and Ch'unbok. In the criminal cases of Kim Chongwŏn, Ch'undŭk, Chang Se'o, and Sin Sŏngdae were tortured almost to death.

---

[450] Another name for Puryŏng.

KIM RYŎ

222. *Children I Really Miss*

I ask, what do you think
of our beloved northern seaside?
After living for five years on the border,
I came to know some children and loved them dearly.
Mr. Sŏ had two pretty girls,
and Ina and China were twins.
I wonder if fatherless Ch'un'gap and his sister
are well; they were miserable then.
Yŏngdŭg was carefree by nature,
Sŏkp'yŏn and Pangja were good at carrying luggage.
Their plaited ponytails are still vivid to me.
I wonder when I will see them again.

Sŏ Undae had two sons. My neighbor Kim Chinsŏng's two grandchildren were twins. Yŏnhŭi raised Ch'un'gap and his sister. Yŏngdŭg, Sŏkp'yŏn, and Pangja were my neighbors.

223. Ch'a Chŏngse and Chŏn Sunmin's Poetic Talent

I ask, what do you think
of our beloved northern seaside?
Ch'a Chŏngse's poems are graceful,
ringing clear as a golden bell.
People compared him to Chŏn Sunmin,
but I think he's closer to Hong Sŏngsa.[451]
Someone like Sunmin is hard to find.
He won't go behind anyone's back, even in Seoul,
but because he had no luck until his hair turned grey
he grew old, plowing fields in his straw shoes.
Chŏngse is still young; if he works hard,
his life will not be as miserable as Sunmin's.

Ch'a Chŏngse's other name is Subaek; he is the grandson of Man'gŏl, brother of Ch'a Manung. Chŏn Sunmin's name is Chaekwan; he is a student of Yu Chŏng. He took the state examination nine times but did not pass.

---

[451] Sŏngsa was Hong Kisŏk's other name. See #141.

224. *Evil Officials and Local Powers*

I ask, what do you think
of our beloved northern seaside?
Ongnyŏn garrison clerk Ch'oe, a real rascal,
brought calamity through his cunning tricks and foolish deeds.
He ran wild with that bitch Kim and wildcat Yi,
and let his wicked son manage the warehouse.
He pocketed military foodstuffs, forged documents,
filled thousands of sacks of provisions with sand and half-crushed rice.
Meanwhile the greedy garrison commander
robbed good people of everything they owned.
Soldiers packed their things and fled,
leaving empty more than half of the army registry filled with Hwangbaek.[452]

Ch'oe Ch'anggyu was the clerk at Ongnyŏn garrison, and his son was Ch'unyŏp. Kim Wŏnp'yo and Yi Tongsam were local powers. The garrison commander was Kang Sahŏn.

---

[452] Registering boys and the dead in the army and imposing a cotton tax on their families for refusing to serve during the Chosŏn period.

225. *Winter Dawn*

I ask, what do you think
of our beloved northern seaside?
The snow stopped, the sky was clear, the wind howled.
In the cozy night, the moon rose high and bright in the sky.
In the Ch'ŏnyŏngnu Pavilion, where candles flickered
and the warm wool drapes were drawn,
Yŏnhŭi filtered wine, baked pine mushrooms,
and filled to the brim celadon cups with Yuha wine.[453]
I thanked her, rising to my feet when the cock crowed and
    the moon set.
Yŏnhŭi followed me to the stream to see me off.
Water flowed under the ice, cracking the edges,
and was swept away *taktak taktaktak* into the rapids.

---

[453] A red wine favored by hermits.

226. *So Hyerang's Gift*

I ask, what do you think
of our beloved northern seaside?
A pair of white ivory combs shaped like this ハ,
engraved in back with gold and the front decorated with tortoise shell.
I still think of So Hyerang from Susŏng,[454]
whose taste was impeccable.
A red steppingstone was placed in front of the blue pavilion
and a jade-colored wooden bench was set inside a scarlet silk folding screen.
I visited her house with Yŏngsanok
and spent a wonderful night playing many musical instruments.
She gave me the combs as tokens of her affection.
I repaid her with pretty flower shoes.

So Hyerang is a gisaeng in Susŏng Station. I wrote A Short Story *of So Hyerang. She is also mentioned in* A Short Hidden Story.

---

[454] A placename in Kyŏngsŏng Fortress, where there is a station.

THINKING WINDOW VERSES

227. *An Autumn Night*

I ask, what do you think
of our beloved northern seaside?
The autumn wind makes me lonesome.
When will the long autumn night come to an end?
I remember Mr. Ch'a, an elderly man, visiting me last fall
when hoary dew rose, and the night air was clean.
I read *Namhwagyŏng*[455] with Chŏn Kyŏmik's critical essay,
and you read *One Hundred Letters of Zhu Xi*[456] selected by
    Kyujanggak.[457]
When the wine bubbles in the eastern house,
we let the boy go buy a jar of wine.
Why does the night pass so slowly?
Only stars are cold in the clear sky.

Elderly Ch'a is Ch'a Namgyu. That the book was selected by Kyujanggak means it was compiled by King Chŏngjo himself.

---

[455] 南華經: Another name for *Chuang-tzu*, a Taoist Classic.
[456] 朱書百選: The book was published in 1794 by Kyujanggak. King Chŏngjo selected and edited one hundred letters by Zhu Xi.
[457] Royal library founded by King Chŏngjo.

228. *Chungbong Cho Hyŏn's[458] Shrine*

I ask, what do you think
of our beloved northern seaside?
Cho Hyŏn's shrine in Immyŏng stands desolate
on a bare mountain, its colors faded.
Northerners respect people from the south,
praise Miam,[459] and despise Chungbong.
Who is this grey-haired man in the black hat,
guarding the empty shrine, burning incense?
He bows to me, points to the dead pine trees, the moss-
  covered garden.
He envies Tonggang's shrine in Kongju,
a gorgeous building crowded with scholars.

Miam Yu Hŭich'un's shrine is in Hoeryŏng, and Tongkang Kim Uong's is in Chongsŏng. Kongju is Chongsŏng's other name.

---

[458] 趙憲 (1544~1592): A writer—penname Chungbong—and general of the volunteer army in the Imjin War.
[459] Miam was the penname of Yu Hŭich'un, a writer and civil official in the early Chosŏn period, exiled to Chongsŏng for nineteen years, during which he taught many people.

229. *The Achievement of Minister Yu Hong*

I ask, what do you think
of our beloved northern seaside.
Minster Yu's fame inspires fear in the Kwanbuk people;
his name engraved on stone still shines.
I recall the elder of the cabinet escorting the crown prince up here
when P'yŏngch'u[460] dared to make a fuss in the old days.
The crown prince relied on the minister in the crisis,
and the enemies on our northeastern border were kept out.
China suffered from southern and western plunderers for eight years,
but Emperor Wanli[461] rescued us from imminent ruin.
A wise king and his loyal vassal met as wind and cloud,
and they will enjoy peace forever.

---

[460] 平酋: A derogatory appellation of 豊臣秀吉, Toyotomi Hideyoshi, a Sengoku general and politician who invaded Korea in 1592. His original surname was P'yŏng; Ch'u (酋) means the head of a tribe.

[461] The Wanli Emperor, Zhu Yijun, was the Ming dynasty's fourteenth emperor. "Wanli," the era name of his reign, means "ten thousand calendars." He was the Longqing Emperor's third son.

Lord Yu Hong[462] escorted King Kwanghaegun to Kwanbuk in 1952. Yu's name is engraved on Hyŏngje Rock.

---

[462] 俞泓(1524-1594): A middle Chosŏn period writer who was Hamgyŏng provincial army commander and Hoeryŏng district magistrate. During the Imjin invasion, he escorted the crown prince and the ancestral tablets from the Royal Ancestral Shrine to the northeastern seaboard.

THINKING WINDOW VERSES

230. *Sin Sukchu's Military Feat*

I ask, what do you think
of our beloved northern seaside?
The northern people remember Sin Pŏmong
as a faithful statesman who defeated the barbarians.
He came back to wash his sword on the shore of the Hŭksimha
then marched to Hwangjap'an Field, where horses were feeding.
The moonlight shone gold against the steel armor
of 300,000 soldiers carrying bow cases on their shoulders.
The flowing blood of the defeated barbarians formed a stream,
and the Jurchens fled through Palga under the cover of night.
The three big letters on a gravestone on Mach'ŏllyŏng Pass
will not be worn away, even by thousands of years of wind and rain.

Lord Munch'ung Sin Sukchu's other name was Pŏmong. He became Chŏngho General of the Army (in charge of attacking barbarians) when young. Hwangjap'an is a placename.

231. *Fortuneteller's Divination Sign*

I ask, what do you think
of our beloved northern seaside?
Scholar Ch'ae's fortunetelling was said to be marvelous—
he was deemed the best after Hwang Sangch'ŏng.[463]
The Kaewon Tongbo[464] coins in his pockets
were worn out, their lettering blurred.
He cast coins for me, divining a sign of water and lightning,
which made the year of the chicken auspicious for me.[465]
Barely saving my neck after being flogged, I waited for good fortune,
which never came, and I was sent to the southern border again.
Do I have to wait, believing the fortuneteller's words,
for good news to come in the fall after the worries of spring?

Kokyŏng is other name of Ch'ae Ch'wiro from Kyŏngwŏn. Song Hyŏngjong in the east village is a fortuneteller who divined my fortune one spring. He said there would be worries that spring but joy in the fall, and that the southwestern wind was auspicious.

---

[463] 黃尚淸: A fortuneteller, who studied under Cho Yangnae (1752-1801), a scholar of *The Book of Changes*.
[464] Kaiyuan Tongbao (開元通寶) was a form of currency cast by Tang Gaozu Wude in 621—the longest lasting and most important Tang dynasty currency.
[465] Refers to the year 1801 when, in March, Kim Ryŏ was tortured and exiled to Chinhae.

232. *Im Yojo's Sweet Tongue*

I ask, what do you think
of our beloved northern seaside?
Im Yojo's speaking ability is like that of Sojin and Changŭi.[466]
Her words, flowing like a waterfall, resemble Killyo's.[467]
This year she turned twenty-three,
she's tall and pale, with charming eyebrows.
She casts fetching glances with her clear jade-like pupils,
her cloud-shaped raven hair is smooth as the distant mountains.
She behaved haughtily toward men
until she accepted Sŭng Kim as her husband.
Strumming the geomungo in the moonlight, she says,
"My new song is better than what you hear in the pleasure quarters."

Im Yojo is the third daughter of Im P'al. Sŭng Kim's name is Kim Hajin.

---

[466] 蘇秦 Suqin and 張儀 Zhangyi: Famous orators from the Warring period.
[467] 吉了: A mynah bird.

233. Petty Official Cho Munbyŏk

I ask, what do you think
of our beloved northern seaside?
Among fifty petty officials in Puryŏng
Cho Munbyŏk is the best at writing.
He is of medium height, with an angular forehead and a
    fat torso,
handsome, dark-haired, ruddy-cheeked.
With a six-ch'i[468] short red brush in his hand,
he writes in a very beautiful cursive style of calligraphy.
He comes to the office daily at six
and wakes me with a knock on the door.
I love how upright and clean he is,
how different he is from that cunning Hŭich'un.

Cho Munbyŏk's other name is Hyŏngbaek; he is Yŏnhŭi's maternal cousin. Hŭich'un's family name was Pak, and he was also an official, but he loved complex things.

---

[468] A traditional measure of length. 1 ch'i is about 3.03 cm.

THINKING WINDOW VERSES

234. *A Precious Geomungo*

I ask, what do you think
of our beloved northern seaside?
The paulownia tree in the gap between the rocks grew
straight and hard.
When it was cut down and fashioned into a geomungo, it
had an even sound.
Long ago, I heard that Yi Wolsa,[469] a man of various
experiences,
inherited a precious instrument from the late minister's
house.
Yŏnhŭi, who was hanging out with Ok Kyŏngsŏn at the
time, bought it
for a thousand gold pieces after her bid of a hundred was
turned down.
Beautiful instruments made with good material are rare in
any age.
What number is enough for Kajŏng's cross flute[470] or
Ch'omigŭm's?[471]

---

[469] 李月沙 (1564-1635): Wolsa is Yi Chŏnggwi's penname. He is one of the four best literary figures from the middle period of Chosŭn. He wrote *The Collected Works of Wolsa*.

[470] Passing through Hoikye, Ch'aeong (蔡邕, Cai Yong) in the late Han period, a writer stayed in the Kajong Pavilion, whose bamboo rafters inspired him to make a bamboo cross flute, which had a splendid sound.

[471] The name of Ch'aeong's geomungo. In Wu country, when he heard firewood burning in a kitchen, he knew the wood was excellent and secured remnants of it to make a geomungo. A burnt trace on the instrument inspired its name: Ch'omigŭm, burnt tail geomungo.

KIM RYŎ

When I sang, she played Ayanggok.[472]
When she sang, I played Ponghwanggok.[473]

Lord Munch'ung Yi Chŏnggwi had a precious geomungo. Kyŏngsŏn is a gisaeng of the town. I wrote A Story of Kyŏngsŏn *and* "A Poem on Ok Kyŏngsŏn's Playing of Yi Wolsa's Geomungo Made from a Paulownia Tree Grown in the Gap between the Rocks."

---

[472] A geomungo tune that Paega (伯牙, Bo Ya), a qin player from the Spring and Autumn period or the Warring States period, played for his friend, Chong Chagi (鍾子期, Zhong Ziqi). Paega was a fine geomungo performer. Chong Chagi was the only one who appreciated his music.

[473] A geomungo tune in which a phoenix asks a stork for love. Samasangyŏ (Xima Ziangru, 司馬相如) of the Han dynasty played this tune for T'angmunkun (Zhou Wenjun, 卓文君). She swooned over the song and eloped with him that night.

THINKING WINDOW VERSES

235. *Paeksa Yi Hangbok*[474]

I ask, what do you think
of our beloved northern seaside?
Minister Yi's achievements were outstanding,
his noble words and fidelity, timeless.
His strategy was like Chang Chabang's[475] in the Han dynasty,
his distinguished service like Kwak Pungyang's[476] in the Tang dynasty.
He had the literary gifts of Yŏnhŏ,[477]
and his flame was ten thousand chang[478] long.
He was proved innocent in the Kyech'uk Imprisonment,
and his Ch'ŏllyŏng poem[479] is still handed down among the

---

[474] 李恒福 (1556~1618): A Chosŏn dynasty civil official and Minister of Defense during the Imjin Invasion. Chasang is his other name, and Paeksa is his penname. Opposing the dethronement of the Inmok dowager queen during King Kwanghae's reign, he was sacked and exiled to Pukch'ŏng. He wrote *The Collected Works of Paeksa*.
[475] 張子房, Zhang Zifang, a renowned Han dynasty strategist and statesman. His name is Zhang Liang, and Zifang is his other name.
[476] 郭汾陽, Guo Yuyang: Refers to Guo Ziyi, the Tang dynasty general who put down the An Jushan Rebellion.
[477] Refers to the great Yŏnhŏ writers of Tang Emperor Xuanzong's reign, Lord Yŏnkuk (燕國, Yanguo), Chang Yŏl (張說, Zhang Yue), Lord Hŏkuk (許國, Guguo), and So Chŏng (蘇頲, Su Ting).
[478] A traditional measure of length. One chang is 10 cha, about 3m.
[479] A sijo Yi Hangpok wrote on his way into exile: "Oh, cloud that pauses on the high peak of Ch'ullyŏng before passing over. / Why not let the grievous tear of this abandoned vassal float

Kwanbuk people.
Lonely rain on an empty mountain after the leaves fell,
a traveler passing by the shrine shedding tears.

Lord Munch'ung Yi Hangbok was exiled to Pukch'ŏng in the year of Kyech'uk (1613) and died. He wrote his Ch'ŏllyŏng poem at that time. Kwon P'il[480] wrote the quatrain "An Empty Mountain after Leaves Fall."

---

like rain / and sprinkle it on the Royal Palace where my beloved lord lives."
[480] 權韠 (1569-1612): A writer who studied under Songgang Chŏng Ch'ŏl. Line 11— "Lonely rainfall on an empty mountain after the leaves fell" (空山落木蕭蕭雨)—comes from his poem "A Feeling I Received, Passing Chŏng Songgang's Grave." Kim Ryŏ seems to have misunderstood the situation.

236. *Peach Blossom*

I ask, what do you think
of our beloved northern seaside?
Of the peach tree's many flower buds
one has brightly blossomed first. When I broke
the bough and picked the blossom to take a closer look,
I saw Yŏnhŭi's dimples when she smiles.
When I tossed it softly to her,
she caught it with both hands and silently gazed at it.
One by one she tore its petals with her white fingers, saying,
"They look like my drunken beloved's red cheeks."
Laughing loudly, I, an unsightly old man, held the pistils
in my hand and compared them to my grey beard.

KIM RYŎ

237. *Three Papers of My Father's Will*

I ask, what do you think
of our beloved northern seaside?
Though my late father warned me to live righteously,
how could I avoid unexpected calamities in this corrupt age?
My dull nature cannot swim with the tide.
Everyone in the world begrudges and envies me.
Yŏn's vassal received no response from the summer hail.[481]
The falsely imprisoned[482] tremble at the sound of a mosquito as if it is thunder.
Unworthy of my father, I was caught in the net,
and hardship always follows me, like shadow and echo.
Where are the three papers of my father's will?
In the autumn field, I cried out to the sky, my tears endlessly falling.

When a military officer confiscated my books and papers, three of my late father's papers were mixed in with them. The contents of the will are recorded in The Chronicle of Yŏnhŭi's Words and Deeds.

---

[481] Ch'uyŏn (鄒衍, Zou Yan) served King Hui of Yan (燕惠王) faithfully but was falsely accused and imprisoned. He cried aloud to the sky when hail fell in May.

[482] 梁獄 (Yangok) in the original text means a Liang dynasty prison—in other words, to be falsely imprisoned. The meaning stems from Ch'uyang (鄒陽, Zou Yang), who was falsely accused, imprisoned, then released after writing to King Liu of Liang.

THINKING WINDOW VERSES

238. *On the Anniversary of My Mother's Death*

I ask, what do you think
of our beloved northern seaside?
Cold rain and snow fell on October 22nd,
which saddened me, since it was the anniversary of my mother's death.
Yŏnhŭi purified herself and prepared food for the ancestral rites,
while I ran to the cold river to cry bitterly.
The sound of my weeping slashed the distant sky;
the moon lost its light, clouds moved in.
My heart ached at the turn of another year;
my mother's anniversary added another sorrow.
Ah, what's worse than this thankless child?
I cried, beating my chest, stamping my feet beside the old stream.

The anniversary of my mother's death is October 22nd. Every year Yŏnhŭi made food for the ancestral rites, and I went to the river to cry—a ritual repeated on the anniversary of my father's death.

239. Hardheaded Pusol[483] Yi

I ask, what do you think
of our beloved northern seaside?
Pusol Yi was Songam's son,
and everyone said, "Like father, like son."
He was hard as a rock, clean as ice,
always careful, as if walking on thin ice.
He was hardheaded, straight-laced as Chamak,[484]
and rigidly obeyed the law.
But punishing his wife and children was excessive.
He resembled the notorious Hwang the stubborn,[485]
not Yi Chibaek and his son Chongham
who were too mean and petty.

Songam's son Pusol Yi is named Ham. I wrote about him in The Story of Pusol Yi. *Hwang the stubborn is named Yusa, whose story is recorded in* The Collected Works of Yi Sojae.

---

[483] A petty official in the local government.
[484] 子莫 Zimo: A counselor in the Lu dynasty, known for his rigidity.
[485] His name was Hwang Sunsŭng, from P'yŏngyang, and he was notoriously stubborn. When he prepared food for the ancestral rites, he forced his wife and maids to gag themselves.

THINKING WINDOW VERSES

240. *Merchants of the North*

I ask, what do you think
of our beloved northern seaside?
Who are the best merchants in Kwanbuk?
Hŭngŏk and Ikt'ae had big names.
They went everywhere,
to Wŏnsan, Kanggyŏng, and Puju.
They counted money not by strings of coins but doe.[486]
With fine horses and wagons laden with goods, they looked
  like lords.
But worldly affairs have their ups and downs.
Their failing business left them saddled with debt,
and now they lead wretched lives,
drunk every day, screaming in the street.

Hŭngŏk is Yi Paengnok's elder cousin. Ikt'ae's family name is Kim. They were brought to ruin and now lead wretched lives. Tŏgwŏn and Wŏnsan north of Ch'ŏllŏng, Ŭnjin and Kanggyŏng in Hosŏ, and Yŏngch'ŏn and Puju in Yŏngnam are large cities.

---

[486] A traditional unit of measure, about 1.8 liters; also the measuring container.

241. *The Ruined Family of Choe Sin*

I ask, what do you think
of our beloved northern seaside?
Ch'oe P'ungam was a pupil of Song Uam,
and his family worked for generations as chief gatekeepers of Kongju.
He spent twenty years politely waiting in his crimson regalia[487]
to be worthy of entering the room with a spear and become a legitimate successor.[488]
When Song Uam was put to death in a terrible disaster, in the year of Kisa,[489]
he wailed at the sky along with Sŏggok.
He was exiled to the south then the north, and his family declined;
his poor descendants were ruined and became servants.
My wise cousin An[490] knew what to do.

---

[487] The meaning of this passage is unclear. A crimson regalia is a metaphor for a teacher, which means he studied devotedly for twenty years under that teacher.

[488] This means that a pupil argues with his teacher to further his learning. When Ha Hyu (何休, He Xiu) was writing three books about *Spring and Autumn* (春秋), his disciple Chŏng Hyŏn (鄭玄, Zheng Xuan) pointed out many errors. Ha Hyu lamented: "He enters my room and strikes me with a spear."

[489] In the year of Kisa (1689), Westerners were expelled, and Southerners regained power while fighting over the designation of the royal concubine Chang's son as the royal first son. After Song Siyŏl, head of the Westerners, sent a written memorial about royal wrongdoings to King Sukchong, he was sent into exile and poisoned to death.

[490] Kim Ryŏ's cousin, An Ch'aek.

THINKING WINDOW VERSES

He paid one hundred gold in ransom to the P'ungsan Fortress and freed them.

The scholar's name is Sin and Sŏkkok is Song Sangmin. They are Uam's students. His descendants grew so desolate they were sold to P'ungsan Fortress. My cousin An freed them when he worked as Pukp'yŏngsa.[491]

---

[491] A sixth-ranked military officer assigned to military camps in Hamgyŏng Province.

242. *Brave General Sin Rip*[492]

I ask, what do you think
of our beloved northern seaside?
Lord Ch'ungjang Sin was Wiji[493] in a previous life,
and his spirit was exactly like the old general's.
Though his Sŏltanhwa[494] and silk robe were covered with blood,
he broke through the lines of the besieging enemy,
riding Chayŏllyu[495] and grasping an oiled steel Chŏm-gangmo.[496]
He must be Chojaryong[497] of Sangsan.
The barbarians, too dumbstruck even to cry out,
still talk about him, sweating hard.
Afterward, whenever he went to war at Onsŏng,
Jurchen chiefs dismounted their horses to pay respect to him.

When Sin Rip was the military commander of Onsŏng, Jurchens were so afraid of him they still talk about him.

---

[492] 申砬 (1547~1592): A military official in the middle period of the Chosŏn dynasty. Ch'ungjang is his posthumous title.
[493] 尉遲 Weichi: General Weichi of the late Sui dynasty, who accomplished great things under King Taizong in the Tang dynasty, after the Sui dynasty collapsed.
[494] 雪團花 Xuetuanhua: A horse as white as snow.
[495] 紫燕騮 Ziyanliu: One of nine fast horses owned by Emperor Xiaowen of the Han dynasty.
[496] 點鋼矛 Diangangmao: Zhang Fei's spear, which was five meters long.
[497] 趙子龍 Zhaozilong: A general in the Three Kingdoms period.

THINKING WINDOW VERSES

243. *A Bowl of Adzuki Bean Gruel on the Winter Solstice*

I ask, what do you think
of our beloved northern seaside?
I still think of the last winter solstice.
Closing the door, I sat by myself to trim the wick
when Yŏnhŭi brought me a bowl of thick adzuki bean gruel,
which looked delicious.
The barley cake balls from Murŭng were small as grapes,
the wild honey from Chongsŏng was fragrant as pine pollen.
She said with a smile, "Border customs are coarse,
and I'm afraid this gruel is inferior to the southern one.
But I pray my love will not forget when he dies
the bowl of adzuki bean gruel he ate when he lived in P'at'aŏm."

Wild honey was produced in Chongsŏng.

244. *An Old Copy of* Taehakchanggu[498]

I ask, what do you think
of our beloved northern seaside?
A Chŭngja's[499] book was handed down in Lord Ch'ungik Cho's[500] family
and my friend, Lord Nam, bound it with a yellow cover.
I remember that when we toured the Sŭnggasa[501] Temple together,
he presented me with a bookcase containing this book.
Lord Nam is dead now, so I cannot meet him;
my eyes water whenever I touch this book.
I have always said that Hŭiik will become a great man
and perhaps I'm fated to pass the book on to him.
Hŭiik, Hŭiik, don't ruin yourself!
Lord Nam would have done the same to you.

Lord Cho's name is T'aech'ae. Lord Nam's name is Sŏnggu, and his

---

[498] 大學章句, Sishu Zhangju, University Chapter Sentence: The book that Chuhi (朱熹, Zhu Xi) annotated in *The Great Learning*.
[499] 曾子 Zhengzi: His original name was Zeng Shen (曾參). He was an influential Chinese philosopher and disciple of Confucius known as the author of *The Great Learning* (大學).
[500] 趙泰采 (1660~1722: A civil servant during King Sukchong's reign. His other name was Yurang, and his penname was Iutang. His posthumous title is Ch'ungik. As one of the four key members of the Old Doctrine, he fought against the Young Doctrine over the investiture of Prince Yŏning as Crown Prince. He was charged with treason and put to death during the Sinim Imprisonment.
[501] A Buddhist temple east of Pibong peak on Mt. Pukhan in Seoul.

other name is Kongjin. He secured the old copy of Taehakchanggu *handed down in Cho's family and gave it to me, and I gave it to Hŭiik.*

245. *My Wife's Letter*

I ask, what do you think
of our beloved northern seaside?
Last fall my wife sent me a letter—
blood and tears in every line.
"I was lonely when you left me
with many young children moving about before my eyes.
My father-in-law's death added to my sorrow,
and now I must rely on my two brothers-in-law."
The world grew more turbulent.
This spring Sŏwŏn[502] was also exiled to the Kwansŏ region.
When I think of your heartbreaking sorrow in my empty
    boudoir,
which reaches to heaven, my bowels seem to melt.

When I was exiled to the north, I received two letters from my wife, which I entrusted to Yŏnhŭi. I do not know what became of them.

---

[502] Penname of Kim Sŏn, Kim Ryŏ's younger brother.

THINKING WINDOW VERSES

246. *Fans My Sister Sent Me*

I ask, what do you think
of our beloved northern seaside?
Two round moon-shaped fans, one clean blue, the other red,
made with silk in a cloud pattern.
My sister made them with blood-red eyes to send me with a letter.
She pitied my exile and worried about the steaming heat.
Yŏnhŭi used the red one to catch butterflies,
I used the blue one to shoo away flies.
The other day Yŏngsanok asked for one,
but Yŏnhŭi refused, hiding hers like treasure.
Playing t'uho[503] with Yŏngsanok, I couldn't score
three rounds in a row, and I lost mine to her.

I played t'uho with Yŏngsanok at Yŏnhŭi's house. I wagered a bet for her whale-eye cup and she for my fan. I lost. But she later sent me the cup.

---

[503] A traditional folk game of throwing blue and red arrows into a jar.

247. Kong Chŏnghyŏn's[504] Medical Book

I ask, what do you think
of our beloved northern seaside?
The greatest man in medicine is Ullim,
a master physician and true scholar no one can compete with.
In his preface, Minister Chang Hongyang[505] noted
that *Susebowŏn* is a book of true scripture to be handed down forever.
I followed the secret prescription of T'ansa
and cherished the book like a priceless antique.
But the special army envoy ordered it to be burned;
Mr.Yŏng's[506] burning of books and scholars could not be crueler.
Even the book on medicinal herbs, which I read with Hŭiik, was burned
to a heap of ashes and scattered to the wind.

I liked T'ansa's secret prescription in the preface Chang Wi wrote to Kong Chŏnghyŏn's Susebowŏn, *recorded in* Ch'anggaru Unofficial History. Ŭigam,[507] *a book of medicinal herbs, which Hŭiik borrowed, was also burned then, along with other books.*

---

[504] 龔廷賢: Tianxian Gong (1522-1619), a Ming dynasty physician. His penname was Ullim; his book, *Susebowŏn* (壽世保元, Shoushi Baoyuan), profoundly shaped Chosŏn medicine.
[505] Refers to Chang Wi (張位, 1538~1605), a Ming dynasty minister and scholar, whose penname was Hongyang.
[506] Mr. Yŏng refers to Emperor Qin. The family name of the royal family of Xin is 嬴 (ying).
[507] 醫鑑, a medical book published by an anonymous writer around 1790.

THINKING WINDOW VERSES

248. *Sŏk Wŏn'gŭk, a Man of the North*

I ask, what do you think
of our beloved northern seaside?
The Sŏk brothers were all handsome,
and I was especially close to Wŏn'gŭk.
He was eight feet tall, with neat features,
bright eyes, wide eyebrows, a large mouth.
Wearing a blue silk k'waeja,[508] with a manho gat string[509] hanging loose,
he put an iron arrow on his black-cow-horn bow.
Mounting a bluish-white horse, clutching a purple bridle,
he lowered his body and shot a bird in flight.
Who but he can be a real man of the north?
His spirit soars when he rides with other people.

The sons of Sŏk family in Wŏnsŏng Yŏnch'ŏn, Yŏch'ŏn, and Ŭich'ŏn. Chunch'ŏn, are all handsome. Chunch'ŏn's other name is Wŏn'gŭk, and he is Yi Chibaek's son-in-law.

---

[508] A sleeveless battle jacket with a long-parted seam in back.
[509] A rough string with no patterns attached to a traditional Korean hat made of horsehair.

KIM RYŎ

249. *General Yun Kwan*

I ask, what do you think
of our beloved northern seaside?
Lord Munsuk Yun Kwan was a famous general in Koryŏ.
When he attacked the barbarians, the border was quiet.
The Mohe people ran away, the Jurchen feared him.
His feat does not rank below that of Sŏ Hŭi.[510]
He planted defeated enemies' flags in Ch'ŏlmungwan
   Fortress
and raised a victory stone on Sŏnch'ullyŏng Pass.
Without him, we would have adopted barbarian ways.
Even now, the barbarians are afraid of us.
The sea looks asleep, and the sky is dressed in silk
under Sijungdae, where he used to command armies.

Munsuk Lord's name was Kwan, and he was chancellor of Koryŏ. He was the first to advance on the northern border. Sŏnch'ullyŏng Pass is on the border of Yŏnggot'ap; Sijungdae and T'onggunsan are in Pukch'ŏng.

---

[510] 徐熙 (942-998), an early Koryŏ diplomat. His other name was Yŏmyun. When the Kitans invaded in 993, he negotiated with the enemy general, Xiao Xunning, and the next year drove away the Jurchens.

THINKING WINDOW VERSES

250. *My Friend, Nam Kongjin, Whom I Met in a Dream*

I ask, what do you think
of our beloved northern seaside?
I still remember my dream from a long night last fall:
Kongjin rode a horse to my old town,
looking the same, with his purple beard and angular face.
Holding hands, we shared our deep friendship.
Pointing at the picture frame between the folding screens,
he dipped the brush, scrawled, and wept.
Didn't you see how sorry I was to be wakened from this dream?
The heartless stream leapt up and sprinkled in vain.
The dove sleeping in a corner of the Paekmullu Pavilion flew away,
the crescent moon was bent like a bow, and clouds spread like silk.

Last fall, Mr. Nam visited me in a dream and changed a framed picture with the calligraphy for "House where you don't want to wake up." This is recorded in Ch'imjŏllok (鍼氊錄).

251. Analects *I Love to Read*

I ask, what do you think
of our beloved northern seaside?
I used to love to read *The Analects of the Old State of Lu*,[511]
revered it like a deity, cherished it like Taeryŏ.[512]
Though there are many books written by disciples of Confucius,
the grave *Springs and Autumns* became my second favorite.
Grandmaster Mang[513] clumsily imitated *The Analects*,
Hŏ Munbo also mimicked them hideously.
Great villains are rampant in every age,
and the misfortune of Confucian scholars is to become barbarians.
I did my best to protect our learning, along with Kyŏngbu.[514]

---

[511] 魯論語: One of the three *Analects* handed down in the Han dynasty. Contemporary versions of it are based on this book.
[512] The name of the bell in the royal shrine of the Zhou dynasty; a national treasure.
[513] Refers to Yangung (揚雄, Yang Xiong) a Han dynasty poet, philosopher, and politician. Because he worked for Wang Mang (王莽, Wang Mang, a Han dynasty official and consort kin who seized the throne from the Liu family and founded the Xin dynasty), Zhu Xi called him grandmaster Mang (莽大夫). He wrote *Pŏbŏn* (法言, Fayan) in imitation of *The Analects*.
[514] 許文父 (1595~1682): His name was Hŏ Muk; Munbo was his other name. A scholar and civilian vassal during King Sukchong's reign, he edited and published *Kiŏn*, a collection of his own works: an unusual practice, since it was a Chosŏn dynasty custom for writers not to publish their own works while still alive; these were edited and published posthumously by their disciples.

THINKING WINDOW VERSES

I hope people remember my love of rites and music, my contempt for barbarians.

Yangung's Pŏbŏn *and Hŏ Muk's* Kiŏn *were imitations of* The Analects.

252. Sŭng Pak's Young Child

I ask, what do you think
of our beloved northern seaside?
Pak's child was seven years old
but he had the spirit of a swift horse.
His eyes were raven black, his eyebrows were pretty,
and his colorful dress against his white skin was beautiful.
Mr. Ma's child was brilliant as jade
and Mr. Sŏ's eldest son was bright.
I relied on Pak as if he was my elder brother,
and the child, my nephew, so to say, is vivid in my eyes.
His father was exiled to the east and I to the south;
miserable is the child left alone!

Sŭng Pak's brothers have no sons. Recently Pak Hongjung took up with Ch'unmae, a gisaeng of the Pu, who gave birth to a handsome boy. Ch'unmae's nephew, Wŏnt'aek, kindly waited on me.

THINKING WINDOW VERSES

253. *General Nam Yi*[515]

I ask, what do you think
of our beloved northern seaside?
General Nam Yi washed his swords
in the clear deep water of the waves rolling into the eastern port.
The rocks of Paektu Mountain stand high in dignity,
the waters of the Tuman River run still.
A great man met his death at the age of twenty;
who will water his horse, grind his sword?
He must have been Kwak P'yoyo[516] in a previous life,
since he is also the king's grandchild, and young.
Without him, the long wall would have collapsed on its own.
The Tuman River lost its luster in vain.

In Tongp'o (an eastern port) and Tae'am are places where General Nam fed his soldiers. He was King Sŏngjong's maternal grandson.

---

[515] A general in the Chosŏn period (1441-1468), he put down Yi Siae's riot (1467), was appointed Minister of Defense at the age of twenty-eight, and met his death because of Yu Chakwang's baseless accusation.

[516] 霍去病 Huo Qubing: A general from the Earlier Han dynasty. With his uncle on his mother's side, he defeated the Huns but died at the age of twenty-four.

KIM RYŎ

254. *Prince Kusŏng, Yi Chun*[517]

I ask, what do you think
of our beloved northern seaside?
Prince Kusŏng is an extraordinary man.
Keeping ten thousand cavalry in his heart, he was faithful
 and loyal.
His chivalrous spirit and fame brought Prince Sillŭng[518] to
 mind,
and his marvelous strategy and secret tactics were like
 General Wi's.[519]
His upward pointing mustaches looked like those of
 Emperor Taizong of Tang;
it is from time immemorial unheard of to become a
 minister in one's twenties.
After distinguished service, he received no reward but was
 killed instead.
Alas, he was reduced to wearing jade jewelry and blue

---

[517] 龜城公子 (1441~1479): Prince Kusŏng, Yi Chun. His father was Yi Ku, the fourth son of King Sejong. When Yi Siae's riot broke out in 1467, he was appointed Commander-in-Chief of the Four Provinces of Hamgyŏng, Kangwon, Pyŏng'an, and Hwanghae, and stopped the riot. In 1470, he was falsely accused of dethroning young King Sŏngjong and exiled to Yŏnghae, Kyŏngsang Province, where he died ten years later.

[518] 信陵君, Lord Xinling, named Muki (無忌, Wuji), was a prominent aristocrat, statesman, and general of the Warring States period and one of the Four Lords of the Warring States.

[519] 衛將軍 General Wei: A military general during the reign of Emperor Wu of Han, he defeated Hyungno (匈奴, Xiongnu) seven times and was promoted to Grand General.

coral.[520]

Even now, when people in the Northern Provinces perform an exorcism,
they look to see if the blue flag on the golden bough shines or not.

Prince Kusŏng, Yi Chun, along with Nam Yi, subjugated Yi Siae. He was poisoned to death.[521] *Whenever people in Northern Provinces perform an exorcism, they hold a memorial service for him. This is recorded in* Yŏngsansinsa (寧山神詞).

---

[520] The royal offspring were left in a miserable state, from Du Fu's "Grieving Royal Offspring 哀王孫)": "Poor as royal offspring wearing jade jewelry, / with blue coral around their waists, and crying in the street!"

[521] Prince Kusŏng was not poisoned but died in exile. It seems that Kim Ryŏ was mistaken.

255. *My Grey Hair Grew Bold*

I ask, what do you think
of our beloved northern seaside?
If you have wings, don't try to reclaim the Bohai sea like
    Chŏngwi,[522]
if you have power, don't try to move the high mountain
    like Lord Wu.[523]
Why did heaven send men of great talents,
also a bunch of people who envy their achievements?
My nine-fold liver and bowels twist nine times a day,
and the blood circulating in my body shakes like thunder.
Snowstorms and sweltering heat occur in the king's
    territory,
and customs vary, just as the earth and sky are different.
My grey hair grew bold, and my teeth fell out.
I look up and see only the running Ot'o.[524]

---

[522] 精衛, Jingwei: A bird in Chinese mythology. Yŏmje's (炎帝 Yandi) daughter Yŏwa (如娃 Nüwa) drowned while playing in the Eastern Sea and changed into a bird. To fill the sea, she always carried a pebble and twigs in her mouth and dropped them into the Eastern Sea; a metaphor for foolish behavior.
[523] 愚公, Yugong: A mythological Chinese figure who tried to move T'aehang Mountain (太行山 Taihang Mountian), which blocked his view. He dug it out with a hoe and a basket. This fable of 愚公移山 (Yugong yishan) emphasizes the virtues of perseverance and willpower.
[524] Literally, crow and rabbit; another name for the sun and moon, derived from the myth that the crow lives in the sun and the rabbit in the moon.

256. Impeached An, My Cousin

I ask, what do you think
of our beloved northern seaside?
An's discerning eye was like a bright hanging mirror,
and he repaid the king's favor with an unchanging heart.
This year many talented people were recommended by konggŏ,[525]
which is like the civil service exam for northern scholars in the years of Hwangu.[526]
Moreover, he ruled the Qing Market uprightly and impartially.
Because he was junior to Censor Yi, Qing people called An their big brother.
The greedy special army envoy had a sly nature;
he was busy slandering and calling for impeachment.[527]
When he raced south with a gilded identity tag,
gripping the horse's head, the town elders wept helplessly.

Censor Yi Tam's other name is Kyŏngnyong and he worked as a minister. Because he set rules for the Qing Market as a Pukp'yŏngsa during King Yŏngjo's reign, Qing people still call him Censor Kyŏngnyong.

---

[525] Selecting a talented rural person to send to Seoul.
[526] 皇祐, Huangyou: The era name of Injong (仁宗, Rensong) of Song, 1049-1053.
[527] Refers to Yi Pyŏngjŏng, who fired Pukp'yŏngsa An Ch'aek when he was Hamgyŏng Provincial Governor in 1801.

257. Yŏnhŭi's Filial Piety

I ask, what do you think
of our beloved northern seaside?
People talk about Yŏnhŭi's beauty and talent,
but I admire her extraordinary filial piety.
She always said, "Stupid Yun, a slave in the administrative
  office,
is much better than the handsome petty official Chang.
One-eyed though he is, no one is more filial north of
  Ch'ollyŏng Pass."
She also said, "If I'm reborn in the next world,
I don't hope to gain great wealth or fame
but to return as a man who plows fields, catches fish,
and serves his parents, laughing all the time."

Petty official Chang Tŏkchae did not honor his stepmother's will. Yun Tŭngnin, a slave in the administrative office, was stupid but filial.

258. Shrewd Chehal,[528] Kim Sŏkkon

I ask, what do you think
of our beloved northern seaside?
How resentful is Chehal Kim living south of the fortress!
You should be distant outwardly and affectionate inwardly
    to such a shrewd man.
He won the special favor of Pukp'yŏngsa last winter,
but slandered and falsely accused him to the provincial
    office.
You raised a tiger and brought calamity to your house;
you can neither bite off your naval[529] nor find someone to
    bind your tongue.[530]
I'm not usually slandered, flattered, or envied,
so why did he do that to me?
I'd like to say a word to those in high authority
whose cunning is faithful counsel, their shrewdness,
    stupidity.

Chehal's name is Sŏkkon. At first, he was very friendly to me. Last winter, he committed a crime and was punished, but my cousin, An, saved his life. Not long after he dug up secret information and reported it to the provincial office.

---

[528] A petty official in the local government.
[529] Hunters find musk deer thanks to the musk contained in their naval. After being captured, they try in vain to bite off their naval.
[530] From "ŎK (抑), Yi)" in *Book of Odes*: Don't speak out freely or recklessly. No one is there to hold your tongue. Don't speak thoughtlessly."

259. *General Cho Kyu*

I ask, what do you think
of our beloved northern seaside.
General Cho struggled hard but died.
Alas, his body was entrusted to a lonely grave by the river.
The sunlight was dim in Tongkwanjin Garrison,
which the enemies encircled three times, like swarming ants.
He drove his horse through many lines of besiegers,
kicking the ground like a soaring swallow, turning round
   and round.
The dagger in his hand shone bright,
and he fought off packs of dog-like enemies.
Helplessly, he made up his mind to sacrifice his life.
His heroism inspires these useless tears.

The royal servant Cho Kyu died during the riot of Yi Siae and was commemorated at the ceremonial gate. I wrote "The Epigraph of Assistant Prefect, Lord Cho" separately.

THINKING WINDOW VERSES

260. *Commander-in-Chief Wŏn Kyun*

I ask, what do you think
of our beloved northern seaside?
Commander-in-Chief Wŏn Kyun was so imposing
that mere rumors of his presence caused the barbarian
    leader to lose his spirit.
With a rectangular face and white skin,
this brave man easily pulled three stone arrows at a time.
When he caught a tiger in the mountains above Sŏp'yŏng
    valley,
trees and plants turned red with its blood.
He was born with enormous strength, not wisdom;
alas, he lost his fame in the southern sea.
Wŏn Kyun, Wŏn Kyun, you are misguided.
Your talent is no match for Lord Ch'ungmu.

When Commander-in-Chief Wŏn Kyun was in Puryŏng, the barbarians at the border shook with fear. I wrote The Story of Commander-in-Chief Wŏn Kyun. *Sŏpyŏng is a placename. Lord Ch'ungmu is General Yi Sunsin.*

KIM RYŎ

261. *My Students*

I ask, what do you think
of our beloved northern seaside?
There were so many talented children in Puch'un,
and I can't forget those who studied under me.
Clear and pure Yŏllyang diligently memorized poetry,
elegant Yeyŏ struggled hard at writing,
Pak Ch'unsu's beautiful child was like a phoenix chick,
Chesŏn's son resembled a dragon risen from a stream.
If they work hard, they have the potential to become great scholars;
they never yielded the place of top scholar to anybody.
But this net covering the world is stifling.
I reflect silently on old memories and give in to useless sadness.

Kim Yiin's other name is Yŏllyang, and Yeyŏ is Ch'a Kyŏngno. Pak Ch'unsu's son, Munsik's other name is Hoeji, and Yang Chesŏn's other name is Ch' ŏllok.

262. *An Awakening Word*

I ask, what do you think
of our beloved northern seaside?
I think the similarity between Yŏwŏnmyŏng[531] and Yi Yi[532]
is that they didn't discriminate against anyone.
I hear an awakening word from Yŏnhŭi:
"Scrutinize thoroughly to clear up dubious or vague points."
This came from her reading; it asks me to think deeply
and not to misinterpret a word or half-phrase.
The words were in my brother Sŏwon's burned bamboo container;
similar words can also be found on the inkstone.
How can we sit together touching knees while we are still alive?
How can we be wakened like others and enter the realm of enlightenment?

My earlier discussion of Yŏwŏnmyŏng with Yŏnhŭi is recorded in Yŏnhŭi's Words and Deeds.

---

[531] 呂原明. Lu Yuanming (1039~1116): Hŭich'ŏl (希哲, Xizhe) is his name; Wonmyŏng is his other name. A well-known statesman and scholar during the reign of Emperor Zhezong of Song.
[532] 李耳: The name of Laozi, the reputed author of *Tao Te Ching* and founder of philosophical Taoism.

263. The Whale-Eye Cup That Sanok Gave Me[533]

I ask, what do you think
of our beloved northern seaside?
The whale-eye cup is larger than the clam,
and its long neck looks like the neck of a goose.
Last winter, when the snow stopped and the dizzy clouds cleared,
Yŏngsanok asked me to go look at the moon.
"The night air is cold—where would be a good place?
The attic in my house is deep and wintersweet blossoms."
Sanok raised her voice to sing and offered me wine,
Simhong wished me longevity, passing the cup around.
Sad thoughts struck me after such a happy time and tears fell.
How did I meet nice people like you in this dead-end?

I made a bet with Sanok for a whale-eye cup and didn't win. Later, while we were enjoying the moon, she gave it to me. I repaid her with a martin arm warmer trimmed with black silk.

---

[533] See also #246

THINKING WINDOW VERSES

264. *Kim Sŏnsin's*[534] *Letters*

I ask, what do you think
of our beloved northern seaside?
During the four years when I didn't see Kyeryang,
I read a basketful of letters he sent to me.
With his warm heart and high loyalty, he was like a brother to me.
Tears wet my mustaches, when I read his letters.
I tried to erase the name with a water-dipped brush,
because I feared they might provide a good reason for someone.
This spring, a military cadre took away all the letters,
which angered the chief border inspector.
Alas! All my disciples were imprisoned
and tortured, pleading their innocence in vain to heaven.

My friend Kim Sŏnsin's other name is Kyeryang. With the letters from which I erased their names, Yi Pyŏngjŏng tortured Ŭngya and Hŭik. This is recorded in Kamdamilgi.

---

[534] 金善臣 (1775~?): His penname was Ch'ŏngsan. A talented poet, he was a childhood friend of Kim Ryŏ and would send brushes and papers to Puryŏng, Kim's place in exile. He visited Japan and China on diplomatic delegations. His works were published as *The Posthumous Works of Ch'ŏngsan* (清山遺藁).

265. *My Friends in Puryŏng*

I ask, what do you think
of our beloved northern seaside?
I can't stop longing for the Puryŏng people.
I try to forget them, but I can't; they still haunt me.
Pure Sŭng Pak, generous old man Ch'a,
dull-witted old man Yi, elegant elder Kim,
they were always bickering with one another.
There were also two petty officials in Ch'ŏngam.
Like tangerine and acorn trees mixed,
bearing red, black, sweet, and bitter fruit in the fall,
we didn't mind small and large shortcomings
but liked one another and were very close.

They were Pak Hongjung, Ch'a Namgyu, T'aeso (Yi Chibaek), Kyŏnghoe (Kim T'aeyo). The two petty officials were Kim Ihwa and Kim Sanggi.

THINKING WINDOW VERSES

266. *A Military Cadre, Cho Wŏnsin*

I ask, what do you think
of our beloved northern seaside?
Miserable is Cho Wŏnsin, a company commander in Musu!
If you investigate his family, it's splendid.
When his grandfather was a regional military commander,
his grandmother, Miryang, served him.
Right after his father was born, his grandfather passed away,
and his helpless father was driven to live on the border.
Now his father is old, and his own hair is turning grey;
he can't help but grow old on the border.
The Han River flows peacefully by, Mt. Mongmyŏk stands tall,
and every day he stares at the road to Seoul.

When Cho Ipyŏk from Sunch'ang was a regional military commander here, he loved Mirang, a gisaeng, who bore him a son, T'aesang. His grandson, Wŏnsin, is a military cadre of the fortress. Musu is a placename.

267. A Heavy Snowstorm

I ask, what do you think
of our beloved northern seaside?
Last winter ten thousand kil of snow fell,
burying the whole town, and the ridges of roofs collapsed.
When I tried to push the door open at dawn, it didn't budge.
I grew dizzy and felt, frankly, lost and abandoned.
Suddenly the bell rang to signal the roads were clear,
and Kukpo brought me a bottle of wine.
Tamsu and Chŏnong appeared one after another
and cut boiled pork with a sharp knife.
They made me forget the pain of exile.
I drank and drank, singing like a lunatic.

Chŏnong's name is Sŏngnul, and his other name is Chamok. A petty official in the barracks, he was a fine calligrapher.

THINKING WINDOW VERSES

268. *Kiwi[535] Yang, a Loser*

I ask, what do you think
of our beloved northern seaside?
Kiwi Yang was a heaven-sent loser.
He grew up in a wealthy family,
bet three hundred coins in a game of chŏp'o,[536]
with a swift falcon on his leather wristband and an excellent horse in the stable.
He married a gisaeng from Myŏngch'ŏn,
who was young and beautiful with hair like cicada wings.
But he squandered his fortune, became a horse trader
renowned for fist fighting and kicking.
After beating up many people on the road to Hŏgowŏn,
he hasn't ventured north for three months.

Kiwi Yang's name is Ch'ŏnbong. He is a loser who beat up a hundred Chinese merchants on the road to Hŏgowŏn, north of Puryŏng.

---

[535] A low-ranking military official.
[536] A form of gambling played with five sticks of wood.

269. *Spending a Cold Autumn in a Southern Exile*

I ask, what do you think
of our beloved northern seaside?
Autumn came but I only have one set of linen clothes.
It's cold and heavy frost fell; my homesickness never ends.
Northerners fear winter, southerners, summer;
winter brings snow and cold wind, summer, sizzling sun.
How could I know my southern place of exile would be a
 desolate poisonous sea?
Weather is more severe here than where Ch'ongnyong[537]
 casts light.
I remember wearing a camel coat and hat and drawing the
 curtains tight
in a warm room in the Ch'ŏnyŏngnu Pavilion last winter.
The sorrow and joy of the world change in a flash;
how can Sanggussi's[538] pleasure last forever?

---

[537] 燭龍: A legendary god. He lives in a cold region beyond the northwestern sea where no sun shines. With a human face and the red body of a snake, he is said to hold a candle in his mouth and cast light to the world.

[538] 爽鳩氏, Shuangjiussi: A legendary figure who first ruled the Qi dynasty during the reign of Shaohao (少皞氏). Duke Jing of Qi (齊景公), happy after drinking, asked, "If men of old had not died, what would happen to their pleasure?" Yan Ying (晏子) replied, "If they hadn't died, our present pleasure would have been theirs, and you would not enjoy it. After the death of Shuangjiushi, many kings ruled the country before you. If he hadn't died, this pleasure would be his and not yours."
春秋左傳昭公 20 年

270. *Yŏnhŭi's Advice*

I ask, what do you think
of our beloved northern seaside?
She advised me not to be so impatient about injustice
and warned of impending disaster, pointing to the southern sky;
"Dark clouds and heavy rain are difficult to predict,
and they can cause unexpected calamity."
She used to say, "That Changgongye[539] carved the letter for 'patience'
one hundred times was not merely a tactic for ruling his household."
I considered her counsel a golden remedy;
even ten thousand oxen would not pull my heart away.
Bitter, I burst into tears, and my heart went blank.
I wish I could grow old without thinking about Yŏnhŭi in this strange place.

Yŏnhŭi wrote A Paean to Changgongye. *Details are recorded in my* Record of Yŏnhŭi's Deeds and Sayings.

---

[539] 張公藝 Zhang Gongyi: A Tang dynasty character. Nine generations of his family lived in one house. He is said to have carved the letter for "patience" one hundred times—his rule for managing a home.

271. *Mr. Hwang, a Farmhand*

I ask, what do you think
of our beloved northern seaside?
A son of Hwang makes straw sandals and weaves mats,
the one who gave himself to farming at an early age.
Four feet tall, he could barely support himself with the
    bark of trees,
having no parents, wife, or children.
His character was pure
as clean water or flawless jade.
I forced him to accept my gift of a pair of clothes—
the shy boy was quite at a loss.
The next morning, he went to market to sell straw sandals
and sent me his grateful heart in a bottle of wine.

Hwang Tŏksam is Tongsuk's maternal cousin. Modest and poor, he did not marry. When I gave him a pair of clothes, he accepted it only after much hesitation. Suddenly, he brought me a bottle of wine to express his gratitude.

272. *Noh Simhong's New Tone*

I ask, what do you think
of our beloved northern seaside?
Miss Noh suddenly came to mind.
With whom can I compare her beautiful figure?
Wearing jade green hair decorations and rouge on her cheeks,
she put on blue jade earrings.
Her soft lingerie and silk underwear were fragrant.
Though her bones were delicate, she behaved prudently.
When she drank a little Hongno wine,[540]
a dim beautiful halo shone around her, and her cheeks turned peach.
At night, when she held the geomungo aslant and sang,
a lazy cloud and the lean moon envied each other.

Simhong was good at composing new melancholy tunes.

---

[540] Another name for soju.

273. *White Porcelain Wine Bottle*

I ask, what do you think
of our beloved northern seaside?
The white porcelain wine bottle was as big as a jar
and filled with Ch'unju distilled from chrysanthemums.
Last summer, Second Censor Oh of Suju[541] sent it to me
    with a delivery man
who travelled one hundred li, and I was deeply moved by
    his friendship.
Then he passed away, and I shed endless tears,
beating my breast when I thought of his life and death.
I kept the bottle on my desk, cherishing
and praising it, knowing it was the gift of love from the
    deceased.
White porcelain wine bottle, white porcelain wine bottle,
    where is it now?
I wander north and south, as if my bowels have been torn
    apart.

---

[541] 愁州: Another name for Hoeryŏng.

THINKING WINDOW VERSES

274. *Thinking of Hŭiik*

I ask, what do you think
of our beloved northern seaside?
I loved Hŭiik like my own child;
on still nights we sat face to face discussing our studies.
After we parted, my heart grew bitter,
I thought of him daily and dreamed of him at night.
Tonight, in a dream, I went to my house,
the full moon soaring above,
and loitered in the garden with a stick.
I crossed a stone-lined stream with Hŭiik,
where fish swam leisurely in the deep water,
and when I woke the moon was full in the blue sky.

There was a stream in the garden of Sŏ Myŏngwŏn's house, lined beautifully on both sides with stone.

275. *Flower Enjoying Club*

I ask, what do you think
of our beloved northern seaside?
I remember the clear sunny day last fall
when I went to the Flower Enjoying Club with Yŏnhŭi,
　Sanok, and others.
Yŏnhŭi sent a servant to Kyŏngsŏng Market to buy
　pheasants
to cook a fat pheasant dish I particularly liked.
The meat of cock and hen pheasants was succulent and
　fragrant;
even the soles of their feet were covered with fancy spotted
　designs.
Dishes of meat marinated in kimchi, radish kimchi, dried
　fish, and blowfish were added.
The dumplings with manna lichen were especially good.
It's hard to endure this place where I write poems before
　the oil lamp.
Who can I console with this agony?

I made a club with Yŏnhŭi, Sanok, Simhong, and Kwanok. Our rule was to gather every spring and fall to drink when apricots and chrysanthemums bloomed. It was called Flower Enjoying Club (賞花禊).

276. Government Office Building in Flames

I ask, what do you think
of our beloved northern seaside?
At the unexpected sound of whistling in the depths of
  night,
all the people in the fortress shouted.
I jumped to my feet and opened the door
to see the government office building in flames.
The hay shed and stables burned one after another,
ridge poles broke, roof tiles blew away in gusts of wind.
Everyone was shouting and pumping water,
while the river flowed on unconcerned.
Lord Hwangjangmok descended from the hall and ran
  away—
he had no time to save his dear woods.

When Yu Sangnyang was a regional military commander, the government office building caught fire. The fire burned one hundred rooms and spread to the nearby civilian houses. The whistle summoning soldiers in the middle of the night was quite loud.

277. *False Beacon*

I ask, what do you think
of our beloved northern seaside?
A smoke signal rose from the beacon fire station
high on Namsŏk Mountain around 12: 45 in the afternoon.
Last spring a wicked man lit a false signal fire,
which the district office didn't notice.
The military governor, shocked, hurried to inspect his troops,
dispatching cavalry scouts to check out the situation.
But the well-connected regional military commander survived.
People still wonder how that happened.
Sons raised in luxury are all sons of bitches and pigs.
How can you deal with everything on the border!

When Yu Sangnyang was a regional military commander, someone lit a false signal fire, and the military governor Chŏng Kwanch'ae[542] summoned soldiers to investigate. I wrote about the incident in Record of Ch'imjŏn.

---

[542] A military official in the late Chosŏn period (1739~?), he commanded armies in the Chŏlla, North Hamgyŏng, and Pyŏngan Provinces.

278. *Seashore Snow Parsley*[543]

I ask, what do you think
of our beloved northern seaside?
I wonder how the seashore snow parsley grows among the
    roof tile gaps
by the tiny well on the south end of Yŏnhŭi's pavilion.
Finding them at Sŏyŏk on a walk wherever my steps led
    me,
I transplanted some and raised them carefully.
Their red agate stems were tough,
and their thick green leaves smelled like hemp.
Yŏnhŭi tied a leaf of it to her silk belt
for the t'uch'o game[544] meeting beforehand.
Sanok was surprised and Simhong was bewildered;
the other group lost in the end.

Yŏnhŭi played t'uch'o with Sanok and Simhong at Sanok's house.
With a leaf of Chuanxiong rhizome, she alone won the first round.
Sŏyŏk is a placename.

---

[543] 江蘺: Another name for Ligusticum striatum, symbol of a wise man.
[544] 鬪草: A game played with cut leaves or flowers in March and April on the lunar calendar. The winner was determined by the toughness, number, and rarity of the leaves.

279. *Treacherous Hwang Pongnae*

I ask, what do you think
of our beloved northern seaside?
He does all sorts of hideous things,
watching others with bloodshot eyes, as if sideways at a sword.
Hyŏnsong and Kyŏngsu are worthless men who gnash their teeth with rage and hatred because of what Pongnae does.
As a pupil of Lord Cha, how can he be excused?
One fish can contaminate a whole river.
Had Hŭiik not clearly explained the last dispute,
this old man might have been sold out.
I have suffered extraordinary blows;
how can my body not wither and fall sick?

Hwang Hyŏnsong and Chang Kyŏngsu are military cadres at the Fortress. They are cunning and shrewd. Hwang Pongnae, Ch'a Namkyu's disciple, is a treacherous person. This thing is recorded in Yŏnŭm Essay.

THINKING WINDOW VERSES

280. *The Irony of Fate*

I ask, what do you think
of our beloved northern seaside?
An old man lost his horse at the border;
there was no place for gain and loss in his heart.
The things of the world are just like this;
no need for an ascetic to worry above one's interest.
Watching Scholar Choe, I finally realized
the Creator's whim is mysterious.
From now on, don't ask me about worries and pleasures;
I have entrusted my fortune and misfortune to what's in heaven.
I don't think anything big will happen to me until I die.
Better to leave it alone and lean over my black cushion.

Chehwa Choe Chŏngch'ang's son, a cavalryman,[545] fell from his horse. The horse died and he injured his leg. He was discharged but reappointed later. After a serious business loss, he went to Seoul and passed the Royal Visitation Military Examination.

---

[545] 親騎衛: A cavalry of people recruited from Hamgyŏng Province to defend the borders in 1684. It later also drew from Hwanghae Province. (See # 282)

KIM RYŎ

281. *A Pair of Ankle Bands*

I ask, what do you think
of our beloved northern seaside?
All the overcoats, underwear, pants, and jackets fit well,
and the summer hemp clothes and winter woolens were
    ready.
Yŏnhŭi suffered mightily as she sewed,
blood trickling from her fingers pricked by needles.
After the soldiers from the State Tribunal took me away,
I didn't have a thread to cover my body,
only a pair of ankle bands, worn and fraying,
which still show off her craftsmanship.
The blue cloud pattern, embroidered with double yarn, is
    beautiful.
I cannot bear to look at them; my bowels feel as if they
    have been cut open.

When I arrived in Chinhae, I had but a pair of cloud-patterned ankle bands left from the clothes I had worn in the north.

THINKING WINDOW VERSES

282. *Pujang Kim, a Rich Man*

I ask, what do you think
of our beloved northern seaside?
Who is the richest man in Puryŏng?
Pujang Kim of Anjin comes first.
His magnificent blue tile roofed house stands high
above mountains and rivers, east of Mt. Ullyong and west
   of Yŏnch' ŏn.
He has many cargo vessels and fishing boats,
and his fertile taro field is huge.
He is also benevolent,
bringing jars of wine to enjoy with others all day long.
They say he makes wine with over a thousand sŏk[546] of
   millet
from his fields in Ch' ŏng'am every year.

Pujang Kim's name is Sŏnjae. A rich man in Kwanbuk, he has two sons, Chŏngt'ae and Chŏngch' ŏl, who are in the cavalry, and we are close friends.

---

[546] A traditional unit of measure, one sŏk is 10 mal, about 144kg.

283. *Drunkard Ch'oe, a Granary Keeper*

I ask, what do you think
of our beloved northern seaside?
Mr. Ch'oe, a granary keeper, was always drunk.
He treated grain and horses as waste and dust.
This tavern in the morning, that one at night—
drunk, he slept anywhere; another drink on credit awaited
   him upon waking.
Oblivious to success or failure, joy and sorrow,
he lived his life alternating between drunkenness and
   sobriety.
I am living the life of an exiled criminal—
a thought that leaves me grieving.
I already asked the smith to make me a spade,
I want to spend the rest of my life like Yuyŏng.[547]

The granary keeper's name is Minch'u; he is the brother-in-law of Ch'a Ijin.

---

[547] 劉伶 Liu Ling: One of the seven sages of the bamboo grove in the Eastern Jin dynasty. A famous drinker, it is said he had someone follow him with a spade to bury him where he died.

THINKING WINDOW VERSES

284. *Kim Chongsŏ, a Giant Tiger*

I ask, what do you think
of our beloved northern seaside?
People don't gather wild herbs deep in the mountains
   where tigers live.
Kim Chŏlchae's feat will be remembered for ten thousand
   generations.
Holding Changp'alsamo,[548] clad in gold-plated armor,
he terrified twenty-four towns in Kwanbuk Province.
When the beacon fire disappeared south of the
   Hŭngnyonggang River,
the cries of the barbarian ghosts were sorrowful in the
   Eastern Sea.
Though his face was dark, he was bold as Paeto,[549]
and his deep righteousness could compete with Pang
   Hoyou.[550]
Thinking strategically, he greatly enlarged our territory,
but readily gave up his life to stay loyal.

Chancellor Kim Chongsŏ occupied six garrisons but lost his life when King Sejo took power.

---

[548] 丈八蛇矛 Zhangbashemao: Zhang Fei's spear, more than three meters in length, was curved like a snake's head.
[549] 裵度 Pei Du: A late Tang dynasty politician, who served four emperors—Xianzong, Muzong, Jingzong, and Wenzong—and tried to suppress powerful military governors and eunuchs.
[550] 方孝孺 Fang Xiaoru: A prominent Confucian scholar of the Jinhua School in the early Ming period. He refused to compose an inaugural address for the Yongle emperor, who had usurped the throne of the Jianwen Emperor, and was executed by the severing of his waist.

285. *Chŏng Towŏn, a Regional Military Commander*

I ask, what do you think
of our beloved northern seaside?
With his dark face, round pupils, and imposing presence,
Regional Military Commander Chŏng is intimidating.
He can easily pull a hundred-kŭn[551] catapult,
he seems like the reincarnation of General Swift from Longxi.[552]
Even the eyes of flying geese and vigilant ospreys are not safe from his arrow.
He hunts roe deer in the field, pheasants at dawn.
With a single arrow he once brought down two birds flying side by side.
Commander Chŏng would make a good general,
No rampant barbarian is a match for him.

The regional military commander's name is Towŏn. I wrote A Text on Military Commander Chŏng *separately. His activities are recorded in* Yihagimun.

---

[551] A traditional measure of weight, one kŭn is about 600g.
[552] A prominent general who distinguished himself during the expedition against the Xiongnu during the reign of Emperor Wu of Han. He had long arms, like a monkey, and was a fine archer. In fear Xiongnu called him, "General Swift of the Han dynasty."

286. *The House We Planned to Build*

I ask, what do you think
of our beloved northern seaside?
I made a firm promise with Konso[553] to cut down
at our leisure the evergreen trees at Karich'on.
Around the peach trees south of the well at Yŏnhŭi's house
was a patch of dry land, clean and safe from loud noise.
It commanded a fine view, with its back to the mountain
 and facing the water;
we planned to put up a few rafters as in a cogon grass-
 thatched house.
When the peach blossoms open next year in late spring
I want to recite a poem to you over wine.
But now I must erase such an idle thought.
When I lean sadly against the bamboo, wretched tears blind
 me.

I promised with Scholar Nam to build a house by the well at Yŏnhŭi's house. We had already leveled the ground but couldn't finish it.

---

[553] Konso is the other name of Nam Hŭngyu.

287. Mr. Hong, a Good Pipe Player

I ask, what do you think
of our beloved northern seaside?
Mr. Hong, who lives west of my house, has a charming face
and plays his pipes with refined artistry.
His clear singing reaches the clouds;
he must be a reincarnation of Sŏlbang's cart-puller.[554]
When he plays his pipes in the pavilion on an autumn night,
even passing cows and horses love to hear it.
But at the roar of the Hadong lion,[555]
people begin to think of him as Wang Kye'u.[556]
A man of refined tastes cannot live out his dream;
his shoulders droop in disappointment whenever he meets someone.

Mr. Hong's name is T'aeyŏn, and his wife is violent. Despite his skill in singing and playing pipes, he cannot participate in celebrity festivals or visit the houses of gisaengs, because of his wife's jealousy.

---

[554] The cart-puller of 薛訪 Xue Fang, a Wei dynasty commander, who was said to be a good singer.

[555] Chen Zao's wife, Mrs. Liu of 河東 Hedong, was a jealous woman. At a party to which Chen had invited important guests, entertainment girls sat beside them, which provoked her to shout and strike the walls with a stick. All the guests departed.

[556] 王季友 Wang Jiyou: A Tang dynasty poet. Though poor, he devoted himself to studying and was upright in character. When his wife left him because of their unbearable poverty, people called him a bad man. But Du Fu, who knew Wang well, defended him, and wrote a poem lamenting the ways of the world.

THINKING WINDOW VERSES

288. *A Drinking Party at Hwang Tŏkhŏn's House*

I ask, what do you think
of our beloved northern seaside?
When pear blossoms fell and white plum blossoms opened,
we chose a night at Hwang's house in Taedong.
The wine in the green jar and red crock was dark,
a lady's carriage arrived in snow flurries, and soft pheasant meat simmered.
There was wild honey for dipping a common wheat oil-and-honey pastry,
a rice ball cake cooked with pine leaves, and bean flour-dipped rice cake.
The host's young singing gisaeng was pretty and mysterious,
with long black hair and a half-smile on her red cheeks.
While she sang songs offering wine in her clear voice,
the full moon flew toward the west and the morning star shone bright.

The other name of Hwang Tŏkhŏn, a clerk in charge of Taedongmi (rice tribute), is Chŏngch'ik. As a grandfather-level relative of Yunjung, he trained military police. Pongsŏk's sister is Ch'unyŏp, a gisaeng of the Fortress. I drank wine one night at his house.

289. *A Fine Cloth Woven by Yŏnhŭi*

I ask, what do you think
of our beloved northern seaside?
Yŏnhŭi wove a pil[557] of muslin with special care,
more beautiful and finer than silk.
She said her poor body was shining
from the red perfume my sister sent her.
She paid ten nyang[558] for thread at Pukye
and lovingly worked the warp and weft.
In three days, she wove forty cha of muslin
to repay my sister's generosity.
But terrible things happened before she could send it.
When I think of that, my throat chokes up even at midnight.

Last winter, my sister sent Yŏnhŭi six bottles of red perfume and a belt. Yŏnhŭi wove for her a pil of fine yellow muslin with twenty threads but failed to send it to her.

---

[557] A traditional unit of measuring cloth, one pil is about 60 x 182 cm.
[558] A traditional unit of counting coins.

THINKING WINDOW VERSES

290. *The Selected Poems of Hwang San'gok*[559]

I ask, what do you think
of our beloved northern seaside?
Ŭngya loved San'gok's regular verse so much
that he personally selected and copied more than a set of
   books of them,
which he cherished more than mongranju,[560]
seldom allowing anyone to borrow them.
He asked me to write a commentary on them.
I couldn't keep my promise but bore them in mind
when this year's calamity inverted the sky and earth
and all my good and bad books were burned in the fire of
   Kon'gang.[561]
Hwang Chŏnggyŏn, Hwang Chŏngkyŏn, a man from the
   Wonu[562] era of North Song,
did the fire god, Hoerok,[563] love the exile?[564]

The five-character and seven-character regular poems of Hwang

---

[559] 黄庭堅, Huang Tingjian (1045~1105). Nojik (魯直 Luzhi) is his other name and San'gok (山谷 Shangu) is his penname. Like his teacher, Su Shi, he is regarded as one of the best Song dynasty poets. He wrote *The Collected Works of San'gok*.
[560] 木難珠: The name of a precious jade.
[561] The fire of Kon'gang (崑岡 Kunkang) means the disastrous fires of war. The phrase comes from Yunjŏng (胤征 Yinzheng) in *Book of History*: "The fires of Kunkang burn all good and bad stones." Kon'gang refers to Mt. Konryun (崑崙 Kunlun).
[562] 元祐 Yuan You: The year name of Song Zhezong (1086~ April, 1094).
[563] 回祿 Huilu: The name of a legendary fire god.
[564] Refers to Hwang Chŏnggyŏn, who was exiled twice.

San'gok that Scholar Kang Sangguk selected were published in two volumes. He asked me to write something about them, and I agreed. But calamity struck even before I could begin.

291. Pak Chunghong Who Sent Me Packets of Herbal Medicine

I ask, what do you think
of our beloved northern seaside?
I am truly thankful to Pak Chunghong of Eastern Village.
He always pitied me and sent packets of medicine.
We promised to dry mulberry leaves in the coming summer
and prepare Pusangjibodan[565] with a selection of clean herbs.
We said, "Let's stop eating smelly meat forever, quit what we like,
breathe like a turtle,[566] and discipline our minds."
Too many troubles in this world, and our relationships come up short.
Suffering in the miasma, my mind is full of anxiety in the fishy evening air.
I stand alone in a forest of ripening yellow tangerines.
Who will knock on my twig door and send me packets of medicine?

Pusangjibodan is the name of a secret medical prescription from Kong Kŭmgok.

---

[565] 扶桑至寶丹: A prescription for dyeing hair black, clearing eyesight, and preventing strokes.
[566] The phrase means to breathe evenly like a turtle. It is said that you can live a long life if you breathe like this—a rule for maintaining one's health from time immemorial.

KIM RYŎ

292. *Munji's Filial Piety*

I ask, what do you think
of our beloved northern seaside?
Sŏngwŏn and Munji[567] were cousins,
their affection was deep, their behavior, upright.
Munji was a better writer than Sŏngwŏn,
and he was soon called Yangwan[568] along with his uncle.
His father drank every day and acted as he pleased,
so he worried, sighed, and served him with all his heart.
This warm heart grew inside until it was revealed in his face;
my cousin An also acknowledged him as a filial son the other day.
Who could imagine we would pull oars together in a dugout canoe
after the spring rains arrived from the Okp'o valley?

Munsŏng's father, Kyŏngbin liked drinking. I rented a small boat and fished salmon with Munsŏng in the Okp'o valley.

---

[567] Sŏngwŏn is Kim Chongguk and Munji is Pak Munsŏng.
[568] 兩阮: Refers to Wan Chŏk (阮籍 Ruan Ji) and Wan Ham (阮咸 Ruan Xian) of the Jin dynasty. Uncle and cousin, they were members of the Seven Sages of the Bamboo Grove.

THINKING WINDOW VERSES

293. *Simhong's Smooth Tongue*

I ask, what do you think
of our beloved northern seaside?
How lovely was Simhong's wise tongue;
her humor was at times eloquent and extraordinary.
When she was drunk at a spring meeting,
the other women smiled and asked her to deliver congratulations:
"I humbly wish our women will reduce sexual desire a little to receive a big blessing this year."
When Sanok asked her to replace "reduce (少) with 'renounce (頓)',"
Simhong laughed and said:
"I'll save 'renounce (頓) for next year'."
A nobleman's words should have such scope.

The gisaengs of the Fortress were beautiful and full of sexual desire, all sisters and relatives of Hongsim.

294. *I Met Yŏnhŭi in a Dream*

I ask, what do you think
of our beloved northern seaside?
What a strange dream I had tonight!
Yŏnhŭi held my hand, weeping,
choking, barely able to speak.
"After my love was arrested and left me,
the cherry and apricot trees by the well
died at the same moment, their roots eaten by worms.
But suddenly this fall there were new buds,
and the branches thickened with leaves.
My love, please come back like the trees
so we can meet again and live together in this life."

My dream of September 6th was quite vivid. My heart ached when I woke.

THINKING WINDOW VERSES

295. *Yŏngsanok's Grudge*

I ask, what do you think
of our beloved northern seaside?
Trapped in her spine-shattering grudge,
Yŏngsanok sheds tears every night, crying,
"When heaven brought forth this miserable body,
why didn't it make me an intelligent man?
My fate as a woman of the street[569] is harsh and cruel.
Who said ssŭmbagawi[570] is bitter but sweeter than water shield?
My life is excruciating pain! That bastard named Yu[571]
must have been my enemy for three past lives."
In the desolate women's quarters,
she grows old, resenting her fate, her green chŏgori[572] and scarlet skirt.

Yŏngsanok lamented day and night that she was not born a man and wrote "Panggahaeng" to express her anger. People who read the poem pitied her.

---

[569] Literally, "roses on the wall and willows on the street," which anyone can cut down.
[570] A species of flowering plant in the family Asteraceae, native to East Asia. Its scientific name is *Ixeridium dentatum*, and its leaves and stems have a bitter taste.
[571] Refers to the regional military commander Yu Sangnyang.
[572] A traditional Korean jacket.

296. *A Memory with Chang Paengnŭng*

I ask, what do you think
of our beloved northern seaside?
Far-sighted though I am, I still know the road to Ch'ŏngam.
Chang Paengnŭng's house has trees at the water's edge.
How lovely, clear, and mysterious are his poems and odes!
He enjoys reading Tongp'a, learning from and imitating
    him.
His taste for the arts has no parallel in any age.
Who will write lovely lyrics and beautiful phrases like him?
I recall having no difficulty crossing the single log bridge
    south of the Yŏngnakchŏng Pavilion in a fierce snowstorm
    last winter.
Happy, we drank in a cozy house of Im Yojo,
sang Yŏngjuak[573] songs, and clapped.

In exile, Yi Kwangsa composed Yŏngjuak, *one hundred seven-character regular lyrics.*

---

[573] Because Yŏngju is the other name of Puryŏng, these songs are about Puryŏng.

THINKING WINDOW VERSES

297. *Chi Tŏkhae, a Literary and Military Man*

I ask, what do you think
of our beloved northern seaside?
Chi Tŏkhae is skilled in both literary and martial arts.
His character is upright, his ambition large.
He doesn't memorize insignificant names in books;
war strategy is always on his mind.
His lifelong wish is to go to Seoul to enjoy himself,
poor as he is and obliged to care for his parents.
My prize student and ageless friend,
he is close to me in spirit.
Chi Tŏkhae, please take care of yourself.
No one is better than you north of Maullyŏng Pass.

Chi Tŏkhae's father, Chi Ch'ujik, is old, and Tŏkhae took his filial obligations seriously.

298. *Missing the North*

I ask, what do you think
of our beloved northern seaside?
Seven months have passed since I was driven south.
No news from the north adds to my worries.
On a quiet night, every mountain and river in Puryŏng
grows more vivid in my eyes.
Even heartless mountains and rivers are like that,
my friends, no need to say anything.
Here by the miasma-covered sea are dark clouds,
and the wind is lonelier with the approach of winter.
Grey-haired, tired of befriending "salt-bakers,"
I stand alone, gazing blankly at the clouds.

Coastal people in the south call salt bakeries "salt houses" and their workers, "salt-bakers."

THINKING WINDOW VERSES

299. *Watching Lotus Flowers*

I ask, what do you think
of our beloved northern seaside?
Thousands of red lotus flowers have opened in the pond,
and I keep looking at them, thinking of Yŏnhŭi.
Of like mind, thought, and love,
we did not envy two flowers blooming on one stem.
But the beloved has turned into the begrudged,
and a good relationship has gone bad.
Mountains and rivers block the land and sky
before which I stand, singing to death my lament of separation.
What sins did I commit in a previous life to suffer so much now?
Yŏnhŭi, Yŏnhŭi, what should I do?

Yi Iltae, my renter in Chinhae, is a salt-baker. In front of his house is a small pond in which lotus flowers bloom every summer.

300. *Though I Make Up My Mind Not to Think*

I ask, what do you think
of our beloved northern seaside?
The more I think, the more I can't stop thinking,
and my soul burns up in sorrow.
Though my soul is ash, I can't stop thinking;
as if mad, drunk, and out of my mind,
I murmur to myself, endlessly circling the four walls,
in agony, as if my bowels have been sliced open.
I can't stop thinking, even with thousands of thoughts;
Now it's time to stop and think no more.
Many attempts have failed, and I begin to think again.
My liver and bowels are on fire, my heart burns up.

Here are three hundred poems in total. They were in no order until Kyŏngt'ak adroitly arranged them.

Afterword

These are the works I wrote in exile: *Kwihyŏngŏsago* (*Writings of Hermit Kwihyŏn*), *Yŏnŭmsup'il* (*Yŏnŭm Essay*), *Yŏnhŭiŏnhaengnok* (*The Chronicle of Yŏnhŭi's Sayings and Doings*), *Ch'allabisa* (*Hidden History of a Moment*), *Ch'imjŏllok* (*Record of an Anxious Man*), *Yŏngsansinsa* (*Story of Puryŏng's Ghosts*), *Puch'ŏnp'ungsokkye* (*Customs of Puch'ŏn*), *Yihagimun* (*Stories Under the Pear Tree*), *Ch'ŏnsumanhansŏ* (*Book of a Thousand Anxieties and Ten Thousand Grudges*), *Hwat'angsŏn'ŏ* (*Additional Works of Hwat'ang*), *Chŏngch'aehwalyogi* (*Humorous Stories of Chŏngch'ae*). *Yŏngsŏngch'ungryolchŏn* (*The Story of Loyal and True Women of Puryŏng Fortress*). *Kamdamsokki* (*Kamdan Sequel*), *Sŏlgoyŏngŏn* (*Poetry from a Shack*). But I lost most of them when I was arrested by soldiers from the Bureau of Crime and dropped them crossing the mountains and hills. Only two books of *Thinking Window Verses*, *Journal of Kamdam*, and the bookcase are left. I made fair copies of them to put into *The Collected Works of Tamjŏng*.[574]

---

[574] Kim Ryŏ edited *Thinking Window Verses* in 1818 when he was the magistrate of Yŏnsan, *Journal of Kamdam* in 1819, and included them in *The Collected Works of Tamjŏng*, which consists of seventeen books in thirty-four volumes that contain not only Kim Ryŏ's texts but those of sixteen other writers (forty-seven pieces) he was associated with. It took him four years to edit the book.

About the Translators

Won-Chung Kim is a professor of English Literature at Sungkyunkwan University in Seoul, Korea, where he teaches contemporary American poetry, ecological literature, and translation. He has published articles on American and Korean poets in *ISLE, Foreign Literature Studies*, and *CLCweb*. *East Asian Ecocriticisms: A Critical Reader*, which he co-edited with Simon Estok, was published in 2013. His *Food Ecology* appeared in 2018. The recipient of the Freeman Fellowship, Daesan Translation Grant, and KLTI Translation Grants, he has translated fourteen books of Korean poetry into English, including *Because of the Rain: A Selection of Korean Zen Poems*, *Cracking the Shell: Three Korean Ecopoets,* and Seungja Choi's *Phone Bells Keep Ringing for Me* (2021 National Translation Award Long List). He has also translated John Muir's *My First Summer in the Sierra* and H. D. Thoreau's *Natural History Essays* into Korean.

Christopher Merrill has published eight collections of poetry, including *Watch Fire*, for which he received the Lavan Younger Poets Award from the Academy of American Poets; many edited volumes and translations; and six books of nonfiction, among them, *Only the Nails Remain: Scenes from the Balkan Wars, Things of the Hidden God: Journey to the Holy Mountain, The Tree of the Doves: Ceremony, Expedition, War,* and *Self-Portrait with Dogwood*. His writings have been translated into nearly forty languages; his journalism appears widely; his honors include a Chevalier des Arts et des Lettres from the French government, numerous translation awards, and fellowships from the John Simon Guggenheim Memorial and Ingram Merrill

Foundations. As director of the International Writing Program at the University of Iowa since 2000, Merrill has conducted cultural diplomacy missions to more than fifty countries.

Hyeonwu Lee received her Ph.D from Sungkyunkwan University, where she studied classical Korean literature with a dissertation titled, "A Study of the Sketch Prose of Lee Ok." She has taught at many universities, including Sungkyunkwan University, and worked as a researcher at Sungkyunkwan University's Center for Humanities and a research professor at Dongguk University's Center for the Cultural Studies. A specialist in classical Korean literature written in Chinese characters, she has translated many classical writers into modern Korean and co-authored *A Study of Literature of the School of Practical Learning* (2012).

Milton Keynes UK
Ingram Content Group UK Ltd.
UKHW010749110624
444053UK00001B/64